THE STORY OF THE ORCHESTRA

THE STORY OF THE ORCHESTRA

**Listen While You Learn About the Instruments,
the Music and the Composers Who Wrote the Music!**

Robert Levine

Illustrated by Meredith Hamilton

**BLACK DOG
& LEVENTHAL
PUBLISHERS**

Orchestra Bob would like to thank Editor William Kiester for having a keen eye and being clever and patient, Factotum Jessica MacMurray for listening well and for her creativity, J.P. Leventhal for having one good idea after another and always being gracious, Dave Hurwitz for being both an encyclopedia and a friend, and Majordomo Paul Harrington for his relentless assistance in the preparation of this manuscript. And let's not forget Illustrator Meredith Hamilton and Designer Edward Miller, who have been key in making this project come to life.

Original Artwork copyright © 2001 by Meredith Hamilton

ISBN: 1-57912-148-9

Library of Congress Cataloging-in-Publication Data

   Levine, Robert T.
The story of the orchestra / Robert T. Levine ; illustrated by Meredith Hamilton.
      p. cm.
            ISBN 1-57912-148-9
1.   Orchestra—Juvenile literature. 2. Musical instruments—Juvenile literature. 3.
Composers—Juvenile literature. [1. Orchestra. 2. Musical instruments. 3. Composers.] I.
          Hamilton, Meredith, ill. II. Title.

ML1200 .l48 2000
784.2—dc21

                                                        00-040393

Cover design: 27.12 Design Ltd.
Book design: Edward Miller

Printed in China

Black Dog & Leventhal Publishers, Inc.
151 West 19th Street
New York, New York 10011

Distributed by
Workman Publishing Company
708 Broadway
New York, New York 10003

h g f e d c b

CONTENTS

"Music is well said to be the speech of angels."
                              -Thomas Carlyle

I'm Orchestra Bob, classical music expert and your guide to the wonderful world of the orchestra. As you read through this book, I'll show up from time to time and point out when to play each track on the CD included with the book. I will explain which track to play and what to listen for, whether it's crashing timpani, a chirping piccolo or a fanfaring trumpet. Each selection is a famous piece of music that features the instrument or composer on the page.

The adventure starts now! Play TRACK 1 while you read the following introduction—and stop the CD when the music ends, so you can be ready the next time I appear. (Don't worry if you forget, you can always go back.) You will hear some exciting music by Wagner who is described on pages 24 and 25.

Play Track 1
to hear Wagner's *Ride of the Valkyries*. This is the moment in grand German opera that everyone finds easy to make fun of: In the mythological world of Wagner's opera *Die Walküre*, nine sisters (yes, the ones wearing horned helmets) on horseback are seen (and heard!) riding on their horses, scooping up fallen heroes. The looks may be silly, but the music is powerful, thrilling and vivid—the galloping of the horses is almost visual in the music.

The Orchestra

You've probably heard more orchestral music than you realize. It is often played on the big (and little) screen to add to the drama and excitement of television and movies from horror films like *Psycho* and futuristic stories like *Star Wars* to humor in Bugs Bunny™ cartoons. Keep your ears open and you will start to notice classical compositions all over the place.

THE BIG AND POWERFUL MUSIC OF THE ORCHESTRA

The first thing people usually notice when they first hear classical music is how BIG it sounds. Big and complicated: There appear to be dozens upon dozens of instruments, and they all seem to be playing different notes, but they still seem to be going in the same direction. How is that?

Well, the fact is there often are over 100 instruments playing, and often they are playing quite differently from one another. Yet they still manage to create such amazing, magical music.

In the pages to come, you will explore the complicated yet fun and exciting world of orchestral music from the earliest beginnings to the orchestra as we know it today. You will learn the different personalities of each instrument and how they need to work together and sometimes how they compete with each other like a huge family to produce a thrilling musical experience.

If this seems confusing to you, don't worry about it. The following chapters and the accompanying CD will make sense of it for you. Just remember that "big" and "complicated" can mean "exciting," and that is exactly what orchestral music is. The master composers that you will hear create happy moods, sad feelings, angry and sometimes disturbing moments by using different instruments, different speeds and changes in volume. The great joy of classical music comes from its ability to make us feel our different emotions. Here you will learn how this music is created and why it has the power to make you happy, sad, tense, relieved and in the end, electrified.

"If music could be translated into human speech,
it would no longer need to exist."
—Ned Rorem

PART 1
THE COMPOSERS

THE IDEAL BAROQUE INSTRUMENTALIST

3rd eye for speed reading

2 left hands

2 right hands

Extra (3rd) left hand for page flipping

THE BAROQUE PERIOD

The Beginning of the Orchestra

The Baroque period of classical music lasted from 1600 to 1750. The art and architecture in this era was complicated, full of carvings of flowers, lots of gold coloring, and exaggerated images of love and tragedy which was reflected in the music. Music was written for and heard only by kings and nobility and the Church during the Baroque period—few "common people" got to hear this new sensation.

Venice, Italy is a city in Europe that has canals for streets and was an important center for Baroque music. The famous St. Mark's Cathedral in Piazza San Marco (Saint Mark's Square) is a good example of how the art and architecture of the period inspired its music. The beautiful and complicated gold arches, made from gluing tiny tiles together (a technique called a mosaic), at the front of the Cathedral stand beneath huge golden towers capped with giant statues of horses that overlook the beautiful and elegant square. The Church wished to dazzle everyone with the splendor of its art—the paintings, sculptures and the architecture of its buildings—and the music heard within had to be just as awesome as the buildings themselves.

Composers wrote music for St. Mark's and placed the musicians in the balconies, near the altar and throughout the church to surround the audience with music. The sound was spectacular and the audience was wowed. This was the beginning of orchestral music.

VIVALDI 1678-1741

The Venetian composer Antonio Vivaldi was not only a priest but also a gifted violinist. He was a violin teacher at a music school for orphaned girls. In his compositions, he was interested in combining orchestral instruments in ways that were new in his time. Since his students played different instruments, the school was the perfect place for him to compose. Whenever he'd have an idea, he'd write it up and have his students play it.

Vivaldi was called the "Red Priest" because of his red hair.

These concerts became famous throughout Europe, and the format of the concertos that he wrote for them became the standard outline for concertos everywhere—they were in three parts (called "movements") that varied from fast, to slow, back to fast.

Fast   Slow   Fast

Vivaldi wrote almost 500 concertos for solo instruments and orchestras, but *The Four Seasons*, a set of four violin concertos, is his best-known composition.

A concerto is a medium-to-long length piece that focuses on a solo instrument or a couple of instruments with an additional small group of instruments playing background for them. *Concerto* means "with accompaniment" in Italian.

Play Track 2
to hear part of Vivaldi's famous *Four Seasons*. This first concerto is called "Spring"—and if you listen closely, you can hear all sorts of wonderful sounds that will remind you of the new leaves, chirping birds and flowers of spring. In the beginning, the orchestra is quiet and happy—as if they're just coming out of a long, cold winter. Listen to the violins and you'll hear little tweeting birds flitting around in trees that have bright, new, green leaves.

BACH 1685-1750

But Italy was not the only place where music was being made during the Baroque period. Johann Sebastian Bach lived in Germany, and even though he is one of the most important composers of all time, the music he composed was mostly unknown until after his death. That's not to say that the Bach name would be unknown for its association with music composition, however, as several of his children became famous composers.

During his lifetime, his genius as an organist was well known. In Thuringia, the region in Germany where his family lived, the name "Bach" was used as a synonym for "musician." People would go to see him with the same enthusiasm as people today go to see jazz pianists. Besides being a brilliant musician, he was—like Vivaldi—a great teacher. *The Well-Tempered Clavier* was written by Bach as a sort of guidebook for keyboard players but became even better known for its beauty and the way it showed off how excellent a player he was.

Bach Wasn't Famous Until 100 Years After He Died! Bach's job was church "cantor," a term which, though it actually means "singer," meant that his main responsibilities were to compose choral and instrumental works, mainly for two churches in Leipzig, and to teach. His great talents were taken for granted; he made just enough of a living to keep his family fed and clothed. In those days, musicians and composers only became "famous" if they traveled; Bach's responsibilities to his big family (21 children!) kept him home. Several of his sons became composers, and if you heard people speak of "Bach" near the end of his life and for the next 50 years, they usually meant either his sons Carl Philipp Emanuel Bach or Wilhelm Friedemann Bach. It wasn't until 100 years after his death that the composer Felix Mendelssohn rediscovered Johann Sebastian Bach's music.

Several years later Beethoven's piano teacher would make Beethoven memorize Bach's important work, *The Well-Tempered Clavier.*

Play Track 3 to hear the first prelude from Bach's *Well-Tempered Clavier.* A clavier is a keyboard, and "well-tempered" means that it was tuned in a way that made it possible for Bach to compose in many different keys. Much of the music that Bach wrote, perhaps including this piece, was intended to be practice exercises for his students—but it's such beautiful music, people today enjoy it still. And you'll notice that as hard as you try, you can never hum it!

THE CLASSICAL MUSIC ERA IN CLASSICAL MUSIC

Music for Everybody, Not Just Kings & Queens

The Classical Era lasted for about 60 years, from 1770 until 1830. In the Baroque period, music was so complicated and full of quick notes and speedy scales that many musicians couldn't even play it. As the Classical Era got underway, composers started writing music that was simpler to play and intended to be beautiful to shopkeepers and schoolteachers, not just kings and queens. They concentrated on musical techniques and music theory. This, after all, was the period in which men like Benjamin Franklin were discovering electricity and founding the United States, and the music heard from orchestras reflected what would come to be known as the Age of Reason.

In the Age of Reason, not only had the music changed, the audience who heard the music had changed as well. By the mid-to-late 1700s orchestral music was no longer just for royal courts and churches. Common people began to attend concerts, and this meant that composers like Haydn, Mozart and Beethoven were able to work for rich people who wanted to patronize the arts, just like the nobility and the Church had done during the Baroque era.

HAYDN 1732-1809

Franz Joseph Haydn, often called "Papa Joe," was an Austrian composer whose music in the Classical Era laid the foundation for those that followed. He was an excellent teacher and taught two of the greatest composers in the world, Mozart and Beethoven. He also wrote 104 symphonies, operas, religious works, numerous concertos and chamber works, which were considered to be "in a quite new, special manner" by people of his time (a big compliment in that era), and his works would still serve as models for composers 100 years after his death.

Haydn became very famous late in life, when he went to London for the series of concerts that would cement his fame. At his good-bye party before leaving for London, Mozart said to him, "This is good-bye. We shall never meet again." Mozart was right, but not for the reason he expected: A year later Haydn received the sad news that Mozart had died. Papa Joe would live almost twenty years longer and write some of his best music in the last part of his life.

'PAPA JOE' HAYDN
"Practice Makes Perfect"

Dubbed "Papa Joe" By His Students. Haydn was nicknamed "Papa Joe" because he was a kind, gentle and father-like figure to his music students.

Haydn saw his music as being composed to calm and comfort so that "the weary and worn, or the man burdened with affairs, may enjoy a few moments of solace and refreshment."

Play Track 4 on the CD to hear Haydn's *Symphony No. 101* or *The Clock*. It starts with the rhythmic plucking of the cello strings (called pizzicato, which is illustrated again on page 43), mimicking the "tic tock" of a clock. This becomes the background for the entire piece and is a good example of how Haydn used sounds from his surroundings for musical inspiration.

MOZART 1756-91

While Haydn's work was both interesting and greatly respected, he did not have the star quality and personality that his friend and student, Wolfgang Amadeus Mozart had. He did not have Mozart's amazing talent either: Mozart was a child prodigy, which means that he had exceptional musical skills when he was very young.

Mozart's Concert Tour of Europe that Today's Rock & Roll Bands Would Envy. Though some rock and roll bands go on long concert tours, Mozart outdid them—his first tour lasted three entire years. In fact, he spent half of his time between the ages of 10 and 15 on the road. In his travels, Mozart didn't only get to show off in concerts and flirt with royalty, he also mastered the musical styles of wherever he went— Italy, England, France and, of course, Austria—and used them in the music that he created.

Once, when Mozart was only six years old, he performed for the Empress of Austria, Maria Theresa, and Princess Marie Antoinette. At the sight of the lovely princess, bold young Mozart turned his attention away from his music and asked her to marry him! But, alas, he was too young and at that time princesses couldn't just marry musicians, no matter how talented they were.

"I write music as a sow piddles."
—Wolfgang Amadeus Mozart

A Child Star, Mozart played the violin well by the age of five and even composed small musical works. A genuine musical genius, he would go on to master the piano and write orchestral and vocal music with incredible ease at a very young age. Some composers, like Beethoven, would complete their impressive compositions with lines crossed out and notes rewritten, where they had changed things along the way and at the last minute. Mozart could sit down and write from memory a work that he had composed entirely in his head!

Play Track 5 on the CD. This piece is the second movement from Mozart's *Eine Kleine Nachtmusik*. The title means "a little night music" in German. Imagine, as you listen, that you are in a garden in the moonlight— and remember that Mozart wrote this music imagining just that.

BEETHOVEN 1770-1827

While Mozart was certainly important to the music of his time, Ludwig van Beethoven was important not only because of his talents but because his music reflected the "reasonable" art and thought of the Classical era. His compositions, such as the *Eroica (Symphony No. 3)* and the *Ninth Symphony*, laid the basis for the age that would follow. His music acted as a bridge between the Classical Era, which he had been born in, and the exciting, bustling drama of the Romantic Era to come.

Not Everyone Liked It at the Time. Some people of his time thought that Beethoven's use of vocals in the orchestra was awful; others found it new and exciting. Over time, though, critics agreed that this was a brilliant work.

The Wild Composer. Beethoven fit the description of the eccentric (meaning wacky and weird) composer perfectly with his flashing eyes and wild hair. And he was totally deaf by the time he wrote the *Ninth Symphony*. What could be worse for a musician than losing his hearing? Yet this awful challenge did not stop Beethoven. During the performance he stood before the players marking time. When it was over, the audience broke out into rowdy applause to show their appreciation, and Beethoven had to be turned around so that he could see their reaction.

"Life can't be all bad when for ten dollars you can buy all the Beethoven Piano Sonatas and listen to them for forty years."
—William F. Buckley

Play Track 6 on the CD, and you'll hear part of one of the most famous pieces of music ever written—you might recognize it. It's the first movement of Beethoven's *Fifth Symphony*. Listen at the beginning as Beethoven starts with the almost scary but simple first notes. Remember that theme, because as the piece goes on, the rhythm and the notes repeat it in many different ways.

Ludwig van Beethoven's famous Ninth Symphony is a great example of how his music was a bridge between the Classical Era and the Romantic Era (described next page): It reflects the Classical Era in its four-movement structure, but it departs completely from any symphony that came before it in a radical way.

The Ninth Symphony was Beethoven's last symphony. A few minutes into the final movement, voices are heard—first a male soloist, then other soloists and an entire chorus. The impact it had on people was impressive.

By halfway through the 19th century, many composers feared that they could never surpass men like Beethoven and Bach.

Explaining to a highway patrol officer:

"You can't possibly hear the last movement of Beethoven's Seventh and go slow." —Oscar Levant, a concert pianist

The Ninth Symphony was Beethoven's last symphony. A few minutes into the final movement, voices are heard—first a male soloist, then other soloists and an entire chorus. The impact it had on people was all the more impressive because by the time it premiered in 1824, Beethoven was deaf.

The chorus for Beethoven's *Ninth* can be sung with 35 singers but often it is done with over 100! With the human voice singing the poet Friedrich von Schiller's "Ode to Joy," Beethoven was able to impart his message of peace and brotherhood better than any instrument could.

Play Track 7
to hear the beginning of the last movement of Beethoven's *Ninth Symphony*. After a big, complicated, difficult orchestral chord, Beethoven introduces the human voice—first a deep bass voice, then the entire chorus. "Oh friends, not these sounds!" sings the bass, referring to the dissonant music that has come before it. "Let us sing something more pleasant and joyful!" There follows an "Ode to Joy" and brotherhood so stirring that Beethoven realized that instruments alone just wouldn't be enough to fulfill his vision of celebration.

THE ROMANTIC ERA

Classical Music With More Pizzazz & Oompf

Orchestra music had been through a lot by the time the Romantic Era rolled around (1805-1910). It had been ornate and full of notes in the Baroque period and then simpler and more thoughtful in the Classical Era. Composers in the Romantic Era welcomed lessons from both of those periods and took music in a totally new direction, filling it with astounding passion and exciting drama. They used music to overwhelm their listeners with emotion, writing sad, sweeping pieces about love and heartbreak and magical fantasies about goblins, witches and swans.

The orchestra was also influenced by innovations in the Romantic Era. For example, composer and conductor Carl Maria von Weber designed the standard seating arrangement for the orchestra, and he was the first to conduct from a podium using a baton (previously, conductors did their work typically from a keyboard or by keeping beat with a staff). These changes more or less are still seen in modern orchestras.

Misc. Percussion

Trumpets Trombones Tubas

French Horns

Clarinets/ Saxophones

Bassoons

Flutes

Oboes

2nd Violins

Violas

Harps

1st Violins

Cellos

Double Basses

ORCHESTRA SEATING

But it was not only in the music and music's techniques that the Romantic Era influenced the music we hear today. With the audience expanding from churchgoers and nobility to a larger, more diverse one, composers and musicians started to become stars in the same way that actors and rock performers are famous today.

Like rock stars of today, classical musicians of this era often had women fainting or tossing jewelry onto the stage when they performed.

WAGNER 1813-83

Born in 1813, Richard Wagner grew up surrounded by the theater, and he was already writing plays in his early teens. It was through the theater that he was led to music, as he found his plays needed music, so he learned composition.

Wagner's first musical works were written when he was sixteen, and his first opera was completed when he was twenty. Over a period of more than 20 years, he spent time writing the words and music to a 4-opera, 16-hour cycle of operas based on Nordic and Germanic sagas, called *The Ring of the Nibelung.*

Often Wagner would borrow money from people and be outraged that they expected a "genius" like himself to pay it back!

In The *Ring of the Nibelung* an evil dwarf steals the gold from the river Rhine and with it can rule the universe; the king of the gods, Wotan, gets it back, but it is cursed. Through the four operas, we meet Wotan's goddess-warrior daughters, the Valkyries (one of whom is Brünnhilde and all of whom are usually depicted wearing helmets and breastplates), his mortal children, Sieglinde and the hero Siegmund who will somehow save the world. It is an epic work, difficult, but worth getting to know—the story is as fascinating as the music!

Throughout his life the self-centered, egomaniacal Wagner had many patrons, but his most important supporter was King Ludwig II of Bavaria. "Mad King Ludwig" was as enthusiastic for Wagner's music as he was crazy. So enthusiastic was the King that in one of his amazing, fairy-tale castles in the Bavarian Alps (upon which Sleeping Beauty's castle at Disneyland was modeled) there are entire rooms decorated in the themes from Wagner's early opera, *Lohengrin*.

The Bayreuth theater in Bayreuth, Germany was built to Wagner's specifications, with, for one thing, a covered orchestra pit, so the players could play as comfortably and loudly as they wished without drowning out the singers. Wagner invariably used huge orchestral forces and the power of his music is undiminished to this day.

The Bayreuth Festival, which the King funded, and which still continues to this day in the German town that bears its name, was where Wagner premiered some of his greatest works, such as the complete 16-hour Ring cycle, actually a series of four operas with an ongoing plot and the same characters as his last opera, *Parsifal*.

In the introduction you played **Track 1** to hear Wagner's *Ride of the Valkyries*. Play it again now that you know more about him and imagine the warrior women, with horns, stampeding.

TCHAIKOVSKY 1840-93

Romantic music was also especially imaginative. Before then, composers would never have dreamed of writing music with stories of witches and magic and fairies. But Russian composer Pyotr Ilich Tchaikovsky wrote music that was wildly creative about fanciful stories. Some of his best pieces were written for the ballet: *The Nutcracker* and *Swan Lake.* The *Nutcracker* is about an actual nutcracker that comes to life, enchanting a little girl on Christmas Eve.

As composers became stars they were more able to express their own ideas to the audience. Their patrons could no longer control the messages that were put into the music. Yet, despite all of the changes in the audience, the styles of music and the way the music was presented, composers found themselves intimidated by the great compositions that had come before them.

Swan Lake **is** about a Prince, Siegfried, who, while out hunting swans with his friends, falls in love with Princess Odette, who, along with her friends have been bewitched by her evil stepmother and an evil magician and turned into a flock of swans. The magician sends the evil swan Odile to a ball to which the Prince has invited Odette, and because Odile is disguised as Odette, the Prince falls in love and promises himself to the wrong swan/princess. In the ballet's last act, the heartbroken swan/princess Odette dies in the arms of the Prince, who realizes too late that he has been fooled by the evil magician. Of course, the dancing is more important than the plot itself—and audiences the world over have loved watching ballerinas impersonate exquisite swans while dancing to Tchaikovsky's gracefully atmospheric music.

Tchaikovsky was very sensitive and a hypochondriac too. This almost ended his career as a conductor, when at a concert early in his career he somehow began to imagine that his head was falling off! Throughout the piece he held on to his head with one hand while he conducted with the other. Luckily, he stopped having these hallucinations a bit later on and successfully led many of his own compositions.

Play Track 8
to hear part of Tchaikovsky's *Sleeping Beauty.* Along with the *Nutcracker* and *Swan Lake,* this music was written for the ballet. Listen for danceable music—the beginning is an exciting buildup, where the whole orchestra is flexing its muscles before the lovely waltz section starts.

BRAHMS 1833-97

If only Beethoven could hear me now...

Today we picture Johannes Brahms as a big old man with a beard and long gray hair. As a talented young musician, after hearing Beethoven's *Ninth,* Brahms decided that he had to create music of the same quality; otherwise, what was the point? His *First Symphony* turned out to be just that exceptional.

Soon after, people were talking about "The Three Great B's"—Bach, Beethoven and Brahms. Brahms, however, always felt overshadowed by the other two.

During Brahms's time, he was not known to be a nice guy. He once told a group of friends, "If there is anyone here I've failed to insult, I apologize." It would not be surprising if this attitude came from the pressure he felt to create music worthy of his great predecessors.

Romantic composers began to search out new elements to introduce into their music. One way they did this was to use their country's folk melodies and rhythms. Using folk music enabled composers like Weber, Chopin, Liszt and Smetana (to name a few) to come up with sounds that were exotic in the concert hall but familiar nonetheless. This practice helped them differentiate themselves from those who came before. During the 1900s, in the period that has come to be called the Modern era, composers continued to use folk tunes. However, they went even further by incorporating jazz and blues as well as the new and exciting science and technology of the 20th century to expand orchestra music.

Brahms's First Symphony was considered so fine an achievement that one famous critic actually referred to it as "Beethoven's Tenth."

Play Track 9
to hear Johannes Brahms's lively *Hungarian Dance.* Brahms looked at rhythm to be just as important as melody and harmony—see if you can pick out some of the lively rhythms in this exciting piece.

MAHLER 1860-1911

Gustav Mahler bridged the gap between the Romantic Era and the Modern era. His music has the power and emotional feel of music of the Romantic era, yet also contains clashing harmonies that was further developed by composers who followed him.

Gustav Mahler's music teachers encouraged him to compose, but since his initial efforts were frustrating (and he was not very successful), he took a break from composing to become a conductor.

Mahler's final compositions, the *Ninth* and *Tenth* symphonies and the song cycle *Das Lied von der Erde* reflect a subject that was very seriously on his mind: death.

Among the things that made Mahler famous as a conductor was the manner in which he so thoroughly prepared the orchestra. At this time, many other conductors thought that long periods of rehearsal got in the way of a performance, and unsurprisingly Mahler became known as somewhat of a difficult boss. His musicians were not used to the sort of rigorous practice he demanded!

Eventually he was appointed principal conductor of the Vienna State Orchestra 1897. This was the highest post of Europe's top musical establishment, yet despite the stature it gave him, he still faced never-ending battles with musicians, singers and critics. Regardless, Mahler managed to raise the musical and dramatic standards to heights that had never before been achieved there.

Play Track 10
to hear Mahler's *Symphony No. 4*. It is one of his most optimistic works and the opening movement with its lovely jingling sounds reminds us of a child's music box. The playful melody of the flutes and the bells bring to mind a lovely stroll through the countryside and show how strongly Mahler was influenced by folk music.

After a decade of holding this challenging post in Vienna, Mahler moved to New York to conduct the Metropolitan Opera. Although the Met was quite new at this time, there were no fewer conflicts involved in leading the institution. Nevertheless, he became an important figure in New York.

Mahler wrote his compositions with a huge orchestra in mind. Both his *Second* and *Eighth* Symphonies require gigantic choruses as well as orchestral players, and the *Eighth* is known as The Symphony of a Thousand—for obvious reasons!

Mahler's compositions tend to be very emotional and full of drastic contrasts: quick alterations of loud and soft or high and low; instruments screaming at the extremes of their range; moments of subtle beauty, rage and torment, desolation or triumph.

Although he composed throughout his career as a conductor, Gustav Mahler's music was rarely heard during his lifetime or for the next 40 years. In the 1950s Leonard Bernstein, who became conductor of the New York Philharmonic (the last place that Mahler had conducted before he returned to Europe in 1911), discovered a soulmate in his predecessor, and the New York Philharmonic's performances of Mahler's works brought new attention to this music. Bernstein wrote that Mahler was the "spiritual prophet" of the twentieth century.

THE MODERN ERA

A Mix of Many Kinds of Music

Orchestra music has gone through many changes in the last hundred years. Composers have gone in a million different directions, exploring new kinds of music, new instruments, and new ways of writing and performing. Some composers turned to European painting and poetry for inspiration, others looked to American cowboys and mountain ranges. As a result, orchestras today have many wonderful and different possibilities when they're deciding what to play. They can play music from the great masters, like Bach and Mozart, or they can explore the endless options that contemporary composers have to offer.

The music of the Modern Era uses elements from every musical period that came before. It borrows from popular music like jazz, blues and folk as well as from techniques that did not exist before the turn of the century in order to create music that still causes debate. The important thing to note, though, is that regardless of how controversial it is, orchestral music is still being performed and composed all over the world. It has withstood the test of time, and as composers have created new ideas and techniques, it has influenced all of the other varieties of music one can hear today.

DEBUSSY 1862–1918

Frenchman Claude Debussy began composing music in the 1890s, and he is considered one of the first of the Modern composers.

As a student in Paris he was a friend of many poets and artists. He was a great fan of the poet Edgar Allan Poe and was stimulated by Poe's strange, exotic poetry as well as the work of the misty, dreamy, so-called Impressionist painters like Monet and Renoir. Many feel that Debussy's work is the musical equal of this Impressionist poetry and art.

Combining the ideas of his poet and artist friends along with the exotic music from a tropical island, he invented an entirely new musical language. This included his "whole-tone scale."

In playing the whole-tone scale, the pianist plays every other key from start to finish, which creates a magical, otherworldly, harp-like sound.

Debussy's whole-tone scale is often used in movies and TV when a character has a dream or goes into a trance.

Debussy studied other types of music to help him expand his compositions. He was particularly influenced by gamelan music from Indonesia. It is a kind of music played together by a group of people, much like the classical orchestra that Debussy knew in Europe. The difference, though, is that gamelan orchestras use completely different instruments: Instead of violins or oboes, they use marvelous bells and drums and xylophone-like instruments. Musicians in a gamelan also wear beautiful, brightly-colored costumes and play while sitting on the floor.

Debussy realized, while listening to this exotic music from a visiting gamelan at the Paris Exposition in 1889, that there was more to music than the traditional European ideas. So, for inspiration, he combined the dreamy romance of his Impressionist painter friends, the scary and imaginative poetry of his poet friends and the mysterious Asian rhythms and sounds of the gamelan. The result was an entirely new musical language.

Debussy was a fellow you would recognize in a crowd: He had horns! Born with low bony knobs that protruded from his forehead, he wore his brown hair forward so that it would hang over and cover these knobs.

"In opera, there is always too much singing."
—Claude Debussy

Play Track 11
to hear Debussy's romantic *Arabesque No. 1*. This dreamy music, like a graceful ornament (that's where the word arabesque comes from) seems perfect for the lovely tone of the flute and the fantasy of the harp, although arabesques are usually played on the piano.

STRAVINSKY 1882-1971

Many think that Russian Igor Stravinsky was the most important composer of the 20th century. Like many before him he made his mark with ballet music. Stravinsky made his name at the Ballets Russes in Paris with the music for a ballet based upon the legend of the Firebird. Upon first hearing Stravinsky's music from the Firebird, people were amazed—even horrified—at the sounds he had created, and Stravinsky soon became famous throughout Paris.

"My music is best understood by children and animals."
—Igor Stravinsky

It was his next composition that really made him famous, though. In 1913 *The Rite of Spring* (*Le Sacre du Printemps* in French) premiered, and the reaction to it was quite dramatic. The opening bassoon solo is so high that people could not identify the instrument making the sound, and one critic said  that it sounded like the earth itself was moaning. While today it is one of the most famous openings in classical music, at the time people did not know what to think.

Halfway through Stravinsky's *Rite of Spring*, while the music continued to play, some members of the audience started to riot, as those who hated the music confronted those who loved it.

So great was the passion this music inspired that a well-dressed lady was seen to spit in the face of a demonstrator. After all, those who did not like or understand what they were hearing thought Stravinsky was trying to destroy music. Meanwhile, Debussy, who was in the audience, was trying desperately to get people around him to quiet down so he could hear this revolutionary composition.

Stravinsky was barely able to escape from the hall after the performance. He eventually moved to Hollywood, California, where he lived out the remainder of his life.

"Music, to create harmony, must investigate discord."—Plutarch

Stravinsky did not write many operas, but the one that he did complete was just as original as the rest. The *Rake's Progress* was based on eight paintings by an 18th-century artist named Hogarth and concerned the evil paths in life taken by a guy named Tom Rakewell (a "rake" in 18th-century English is a wicked man). The libretto was written by Chester Kullman and the great English poet W.H. Auden. Since the paintings were done in the 18th century, Stravinsky mixed his very modern music with the formality of Mozart's Classical Era—style giving this work a unique sound and feeling.

SCHOENBERG 1874-1951

$e=mc^2$

12

$m+y=x$

While Stravinsky was in Paris, Arnold Schoenberg was in Austria creating music that went even further astray. While Stravinsky wrote music in which instruments made sounds that people did not expect by playing in unusual keys, Schoenberg wrote music in which the instruments did not seem to play in any key whatsoever.

This kind of music is called "atonal." Atonal music is dissonant, which means it sounds as if all the notes are wrong.

Schoenberg did not stop there. He began using mathematics to decide which notes to play. He called this "12-tone music" or "serialism."

Definition of Key: Certain notes sound good when played together and they start from one note, the key note. The group of notes that create pleasant harmonies is called the key. Schoenberg created music that did not use a key, which makes the notes clash, creating interesting tension.

Music By Numbers. Using a very complex system of mathematics to decide which notes to play (it had to do with the distance between numbers and notes and is very hard to understand, even for some musicians) Schoenberg composed what he called "Serialism" or "12-tone" music. If he used the note "C," for instance, he would not use it again until all the other eleven notes in the scale were used. He decided that his "tunes" would contain all twelve notes all the time—not very singable!

The 20th century was a time of great scientific advancement and experiment, and Schoenberg used scientific ideas to replace instinct. It was as if the Romantic ideas of emotions had been replaced with the Classical ideas of reason, but this time it was reason on steroids!

Throughout his life Schoenberg's music met with hostility from critics, his fellow composers and the public. Wisely, however, he never let this animosity deter his creativity. Late in his life, when he accepted an award for his life's work from the American Academy of the Arts, he said, "The credit must go to my opponents. It was they who really helped me."

During World War II Schoenberg, like Stravinsky, moved to Hollywood, but the two men never met in the ten years they lived there. Since they were both seen as leaders of opposing schools of musical thought, it's likely that they did their best to avoid one another. But it is interesting to note that after Shoenberg died, Stravinsky began to compose using the 12-tone system.

In the early twentieth century composers in Vienna led by Schoenberg, began what became known as the "Second Viennese School." They felt they were picking up where Haydn, Mozart, Beethoven and Brahms had left off in making Vienna the capital of classical music. Meanwhile, in America, the composers Aaron Copland, George Gershwin and others were creating a new music based on the sounds and energy found in the United States. By the middle of the century, mostly because of World War II, but also because of the wealth found here, many of the composers from the "Second Viennese School" had come to the U.S. resulting in a really creative collaboration between Europeans and Americans.

"A song without music is a lot like H_2 without the O."
—Ira Gershwin, George Gershwin's brother

Play Track 13
to hear Shoenberg's *Piano Piece Opus 33A.* This music may seem chaotic, but if you listen to it a few times, eerie patterns may emerge. Listen for themes as the music slithers along to its strange conclusion. You may have to listen more than once to get it!

While many composers came to America to flee the numerous conflicts that occurred in Europe in the 20th century, American-born composers started gaining fame for the first time. George Gershwin and Aaron Copland were two of the earliest Americans to make their marks. Their music expresses the strong, hopeful, optimistic emotions of the American spirit.

GERSHWIN 1898-1937

George Gershwin took music from dance halls and Broadway theater and transformed it into great orchestral music.

His use of American jazz and blues reflected the growing industrial cities, like New York and Boston. America was coming into its own as a world power, and it was the cities that were powering the growth.

Gershwin was a self-taught composer of classical music. After he had become world famous for such works as *Rhapsody in Blue*, he still asked great composers like Maurice Ravel for lessons. Ravel's answer to Gershwin, however, said it all: "Why do you want to become a second-rate Ravel when you're already a first-class Gershwin?"

Rhapsody in Blue is Gershwin's signature piece, and while he wrote it in a remarkably short time (just a few weeks before its debut performance), no other music better describes the America of the early century.

Play Track 14
to hear the beginning of George Gershwin's *American in Paris*. Imagine, as you listen, a brisk walk down a street of Paris on a sunny spring day. Listen as the instruments mimic the sounds of the city: cars honking, birds chirping, busy people bustling around. Gershwin found the whole world musical!

COPLAND 1900-1990

Aaron Copland was the son of Russian-Jewish parents and, like Gershwin, grew up in Brooklyn, New York. He worked to create classical music in which American audiences would recognize their own country.

Copland became a very famous American composer, and his work *Appalachian Spring* won the Pulitzer Prize for Music Composition in 1945.

Aaron Copland's music—especially the music he composed for ballets like *Billy the Kid, Rodeo* and *Appalachian Spring*—is easy to get to know and to like. But early in his career he wrote very tough pieces: When conductor Walter Damrosch led Copland's *Organ Symphony* in New York, he turned to the audience and said "If a young man can write a piece like this at the age of 24, in five years he will be ready to commit murder!"

Copland used jazz rhythms and harmonies and wrote about American subjects such as Billy the Kid. His most famous work is *Appalachian Spring*, but his *Fanfare for the Common Man* is well known because it was used as the theme music for the Olympics when they aired on ABC in the 1970s.

While Copland certainly loved his music, it was not what held all of this attention. Throughout his adult life, Copland had a day job as an insurance executive.

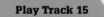

Play Track 15
to hear Aaron Copland's *Fanfare for the Common Man.* Copland uses some instruments by themselves—like the timpani in the very beginning, then the trumpets—to a dramatic effect. Copland, along with a group of other American composers, was asked to write a patriotic fanfare in the summer of 1942 during World War II. This piece was the result—and one of Copland's most heard works.

"There is something about music that keeps its distance even at the moment that it engulfs us."
—Aaron Copland

BERNSTEIN 1918-1990

Leonard Bernstein is probably best known as the conductor of the New York Philharmonic Orchestra, but he was also a gifted pianist and composer. The music he wrote for *West Side Story*, which was later made into a movie, is probably his best-known score.

"Music, of all the arts, stands in a special region, unlit by any star but its own, and utterly without meaning ... except its own."
—Leonard Bernstein

Bernstein picked up where Gershwin left off. He combined elements of bebop and rock with traditional orchestral elements to create music that appealed to modern audiences.

Play Track 16
Leonard Bernstein, people have said, had one foot in classical music and one foot in pop, and this dance music, from his wonderful Broadway musical *West Side Story*, makes use of a master classical composer's ability to orchestrate and a more "contemporary" composer's gift for sharp, finger-snapping rhythms.

PART II

THE ORCHESTRA INSTRUMENTS

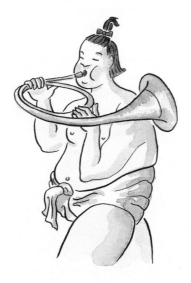

STRING SECTION

Most of the instruments in the string section look alike. The main difference between them is their size, as they are all played in very much the same way; their strings can be plucked (this is called "pizzicato") or made to "sound" with a bow. Strings are used to provide a piece of music with a deep, rich body of sound, and they are often used in solo pieces as well.

The largest section in the orchestra, the string section uses 60 to 70 musicians to create a good, strong sound in the modern orchestra.

In the string section there are five groups of players—the first and second violins, violas, cellos and double basses—as well as the harp and piano.

They are the backbone of the orchestra, and as such, they are so important that they are in the front of the orchestra, nearest to the conductor.

VERY IMPORTANT!

Misc. Percussion

Trumpets Trombones Tubas

French Horns

Clarinets/ Saxophones

Bassoons

Flutes

Oboes

2ⁿᵈ Violins

Violas

1ˢᵗ Violins

Cellos

Harps

Double Basses

Positioned to the left of the conductor, the first violins sit closest to the audience, and the second violins are right behind them. The violas and cellos are to the right of the conductor, with the cellos in front and the violas behind them, though sometimes this is reversed. The double basses are behind the violas also. Finally, there are rarely more than two harpists in an orchestra, and they sit to the left of the conductor in the back behind the second violins. And if a piano is required for a particular piece of music—say, if there is a piano concerto on the program—it is most often put behind the conductor, between him and the audience.

violin   viola   cello   double bass

Play Track 17 to hear the third movement, the Scherzo from Pyotr Tchaikovsky's *Symphony No. 4*. This is the perfect example of pizzicato. The notes are bouncy and quick and quiet. Later an oboe comes in and the woodwinds join in for a few frolicking moments. The woodwinds and the strings have a short conversation—but Tchaikovsky returns to the pizzicato again at the end, when the woodwinds return for the buildup to the joyful ending, where they all play together.

VIOLIN

The Foundation of Classical Music

Max Ernst's model

Violin model

The violin is one of the most versatile and expressive instruments in music. Violins first appeared in Italy in about 1550, replacing an earlier instrument called the "viol."

Where the six-stringed viols were played resting between the musician's knees, the four-stringed violin is played resting under the chin.

While resting between the chin and left shoulder, the expressive tone of a violin is made when the violinist moves the bow back and forth across the strings or when its strings are plucked. Meanwhile, the fingers of the left hand press on the strings to create notes.

The violin's shape is the model for most of the instruments in the string section and is similar to that of the guitar. Though it appears very simple, the violin is composed of over 70 parts. Its hollow body is made of different sorts of springy wood that vibrate, creating the resonance necessary for the violin's sound.

Made from wood and horsehair or nylon, bows vary in size according to the size of the instrument. This works the opposite from what one expects, for the largest of the bowed string instruments, the double bass, uses a shorter bow than the smallest, the violin. While it may be shorter, the double bass's bow is heavier and has thicker strands of horsehair than that of the violin bow. In 1785 François Tourte created a violin bow so perfect that it was taken as the model for his own time, and with few changes it has continued on to this day.

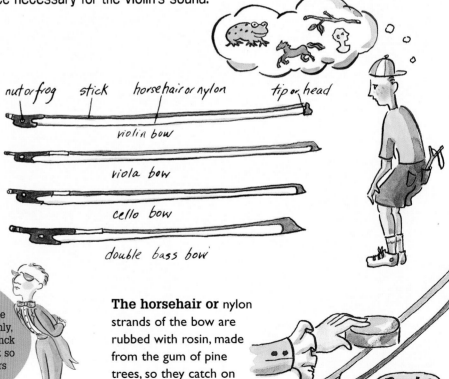

nut or frog   stick   horsehair or nylon   tip or head

violin bow

viola bow

cello bow

double bass bow

Play Track 18
to hear the finale of César Franck's *Sonata for Violin and Piano in A Major*. This section, which is the last out of four, is called Allegretto Poco Mosso, which means "quick, and a little agitated." Listen to how the violin and piano begin sweetly and calmly, repeating each other's themes, and slowly get louder and firmer. Franck composed this piece as a wedding present for a friend, who played it so much and to such receptive audiences that other orchestra members picked it up and adapted it to their instruments—now this sonata is played not just by violinists, but by cellists and flautists as well.

The horsehair or nylon strands of the bow are rubbed with rosin, made from the gum of pine trees, so they catch on the strings and make the vibrations that produce sound.

Rosin

① Stradivarius searched the Dolomites for good wood

② He brought the wood back to his studio

③ One secret of his success may have been his varnish recipe

Antonio Stradivari was an Italian instrument maker who lived in the city of Cremona from 1644 to 1737. He specialized in stringed instruments and created more than 1,000 of them. The violins he made are particularly famous, and about 650 are still around. These are considered to be the finest examples of violins ever made. They are each worth over a million dollars, and many of the world's leading players have chosen to perform on these masterpieces.

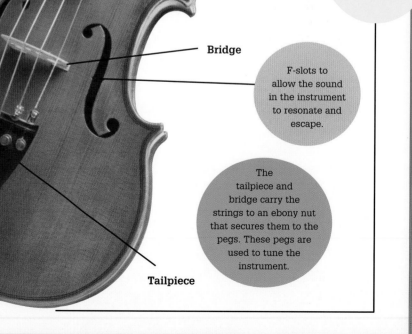

The fingerboard extends beneath the strings along the neck to the peg box.

Ornament al scroll

Peg box

Tuning pegs

The strings themselves run from the tailpiece over a bridge made of maple wood.

Over the body is placed a top plate, or "belly," to which is glued a tailpiece that anchors the strings.

Inside the body, a bass bar is glued to the belly. A soundboard is placed between the belly and the back to stiffen the body and carry vibrations from the bridge throughout the body.

Violins are two feet long, and the higher up along the neck the musician presses the strings, the higher the notes.

Belly

William Shakespeare was born in 1564, about 14 years after the violin was invented.

Bridge

F-slots to allow the sound in the instrument to resonate and escape.

The tailpiece and bridge carry the strings to an ebony nut that secures them to the pegs. These pegs are used to tune the instrument.

Chin rest

Tailpiece

VIOLA

The Violin's Big Brother

Like the violin, the viola has been around since the 1500s. It was firmly established as part of the violin family in 1535, but it was not called a "viola" went it first entered the orchestra, because that word had the more general meaning of any string instrument, plucked or bowed.

During the 1700s, the string ensembles in orchestras began to take the form that we know today, and the violas became fewer in number and more specific in their role than violins. Mozart did much to develop the viola's role, and composers since then have continued to build a repertoire for it.

Violin   Viola

I wish that I had thought of that...

Like the violin, the viola also has four strings and is played with a bow. Where the violin has a singing tone with the highest notes in the string section, the larger viola has a lower tone with darker, more somber notes.

By the 1700s the viola was called "the viola da brazzo," which is why the instrument is known as the *bratsche* by modern German musicians. Since then, as the viola da brazzo's place became established in the string section, it has become shortened to the viola. This was about the time that the tuning fork was invented in Germany (1711) and the steam engine was invented in England (1712).

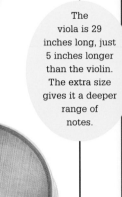

The viola is 29 inches long, just 5 inches longer than the violin. The extra size gives it a deeper range of notes.

Play Track 19
to hear the finale of Béla Bartok's *Concerto for Viola and Orchestra*. Bartok died before he could finish this piece—a student of his, Tibor Serly, finished writing it based on notes that Bartok left behind. The viola comes in right after the orchestra's opening notes, accompanied by woodwinds. Bartok wrote this after he had fled to the United States from his beloved home in Hungary, and his anguish and sadness at leaving comes through in his music, which is sometimes frantic, sometimes excited, sometimes sad.

The violin family makes up almost all of the instruments in the string section and includes the violin, viola, cello and double bass. Over the years there have been several other instruments in this family, but they have fallen out of use in modern orchestras. Nowadays, some conductors use the viol and viola da gamba (the one that is held between the knees) instead of the viola in their orchestras when they play early music because these instruments produce sounds more in keeping with what the early composers actually had intended.

CELLO
The Viola's Big Brother

O ne of the most expressive of all instruments is called the "violoncello," or as most people know it, the cello.

The size of the cello fluctuated in the 1500s and 1600s and most models were much larger than modern instruments. It was the great instrument maker Stradivari who, in about 1710, fixed the cello in its current size. Although it may not be as large as earlier versions of the instrument, a cello is still played by a cellist who sits in a chair to use his or her bow.

The cello is held vertically, with its neck leaning against the musician's shoulder. It was not until the late 1800s that the instrument was used universally with the end pin, or "spike," at its bottom. The spike not only gave the player more security but increased the resonance of the cello that insured the range of expression we have come to know.

Cello is pronounced "chello" because in the Italian language "ce" is said with a "ch."

It's gonna slip... It's gonna slip....

Before the spike was invented, players just gripped the cello between their legs and had to have strong leg muscles to hold it in place.

Play Track 20
to hear the cello lead the opening to Giaocchino Rossini's famous *William Tell Overture*. An overture is a curtain-raiser, which means it usually introduces the audiences to the musical themes of an opera before the singers come on stage and the story begins. The cello plays by itself, in smooth, flowing notes up and down the scale. Occasionally other instruments come in quietly to accompany it, but the cello is the star of this introduction. Listen to the vibrato of this wonderful instrument. Vibrato is the wavering sound that you hear when long notes are held and leaned on, giving them a more vibrant, almost wavering quality.

End pin or spike that holds up the heavy instrument while it is played.

DOUBLE BASS

The Big Mama of the String Section

The double bass often appears in jazz and rock bands, but it is called a "stand-up" bass there.

The original double bass was called the "violone." It was not until the late 1700s, around the time of the American Revolution, that the double bass entered the orchestra.

Double bassists play their instrument similarly to cellists, but they use a higher chair because their instrument is so much bigger. Sometimes they even stand. A modern orchestra usually has at least eight double basses to give the music its deep bass base.

An octave is a series of eight tones in the scale. In singing, it corresponds to "do-re-mi-fa-so-la-ti-do"; the highest note in an octave sounds twice as high as the lowest—it is the same note perceived at a higher pitch.

The early double base was even larger than the one that is used in the orchestra today.

1650

1710

The four-stringed double bass is the largest and lowest-pitched instrument in the violin family.

others ↑
↓ double bass

The strings of the double bass are tuned with brass machines with steel worm-screws; early basses had large wooden pegs. Music for the double bass is written an octave higher than it sounds because it plays notes so low that you'd need a longer piece of paper to write the music where it should actually go on the scale.

Play Track 21
to hear what Camille Saint-Saëns thought an elephant would sound like as orchestral music. First you hear the piano marching a beat, then the double bass comes in, moving slowly and smoothly in rich, deep notes. This piece is part of Saint-Saëns *Carnival of Animals*, where he introduces a whole slew of animals, from hens to elephants to swans.

"If chocolate could sing, it would sound like the double bass."
—Bass Virtuoso Gary Karr

HARP

One of the Oldest Instruments in the Orchestra Family

Harps are in the string section, but they look and are played differently from any of the instruments in the violin family. The concert harp is huge, about 6 feet tall, and has the largest range of all orchestral instruments. While the harp has 47 strings and is plucked like other stringed instruments, it is, however, never bowed like a violin is, so it comes between the string and the percussion families.

The harp is one of the oldest of all instruments, but it's only within the last 150 years that it has become a regular member of the orchestra.

Harpists sit and play with both hands and feet, using the thumb and first three fingers of their hands. Modern concert harps have seven double-action pedals. The double-action mechanism was invented in the 1800s and allows the musician to raise the pitch of the strings.

"Raising the pitch" means that the notes are higher on the scale. The piccolo plays notes with a very high pitch and the tuba plays notes with a very low pitch. You can create a high pitch tone by saying "eeeeeee" and a low tone by saying "ooooooo."

Play Track 22
to hear the *Dance of the Blessed Spirits* by Christoph Willibald Gluck. Here, you'll hear a flute and harp playing soft, lovely music intended for dancing. The harp is often used to suggest dreams, and fantasies—as you can tell by the title, this piece was written to accompany dancing spirits. Gluck wrote it as part of his opera, *Orfeo and Euridice*, which is about a magnificent musician and the sad story of his love for his young wife, who dies.

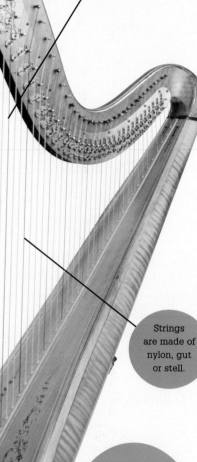

Neck

Some of the strings on the harp are colored so that they are easier for the player to find.

Strings are made of nylon, gut or stell.

It was the invention of double-action pedals that allowed the harp to realize its fullest potential. That is what encouraged composers like Wagner and Tchaikovsky to introduce them into the orchestra, where they've stayed ever since.

Double-action pedals, seven in total

WOODWIND SECTION

All the instruments in the woodwind section are played with "wind" (the musician blows into them). For the most part they look like sticks, though some are longer than others, but they have very different shapes. The different shape and materials of each instrument help create its unique sound.

Woodwinds also vary in how they are played. The flute and piccolo have a hole that the musician blows across. This wind vibrates through the flute creating a sound. The other instruments in this section use a reed. A reed is a narrow strip of cane that vibrates when a player blows on it, creating sound. The clarinet, oboe and bassoon use a reed.

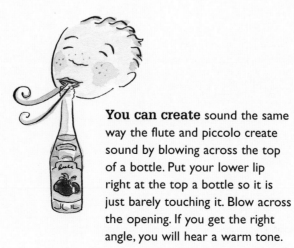

Misc. Percussion

Trumpets Trombones Tubas

French Horns

Clarinets/ Saxophones

Bassoons

Flutes

Oboes

Harps

2nd Violins

1st Violins

Violas

Cellos

Double Basses

Because the woodwind tone carries well and can be easily heard when there are lots of other instruments playing, this section is located in the center of the orchestra. In this section there will usually be two flutes, a piccolo, two oboes, a cor anglais, two clarinets, two bassoons and occasionally, in more contemporary works, a saxophone.

Not all woodwinds are made of wood. They can be made of metal, ivory and even bone.

You can create sound the same way the flute and piccolo create sound by blowing across the top of a bottle. Put your lower lip right at the top a bottle so it is just barely touching it. Blow across the opening. If you get the right angle, you will hear a warm tone.

An instrument like the oboe, cor anglais means English horn in French. Oddly enough, people use its French name in all the countries of the world.

FLUTE &

The flute is an ancient instrument that was played as long ago as Imperial Rome. Its current appearance was created by Theobald Boehm when he redesigned the flute in 1847, about the time the first internal combustion engine, the precursor to the modern car engine, was invented. His redesign gave the instrument a louder and more uniform tone.

A tube just 2 feet long, a flute is usually made of metal.

The standard flute is one of the highest instruments in the orchestra. Its bright, silvery sound is generally heard playing the same notes as the first violins. It breaks into three pieces for carrying and storage.

**Play
Track 23**
to hear Johann Sebastian Bach's *Suite No. 2 for Flute, Strings and Basso Continuo*. This part of the Suite (also called an Overture) is called the Badinerie, a word that composers in Bach's era meant playful. The flute, which moves around the most in this piece, can be played quickly, hopping around from note to note, or more slowly. Either way, the flautist (alternately called a "flutist," and, of course, meaning the same thing—it depends on the "flautist/flutist"!) must have extraordinary control of his or her breath.

The flute often appears as magical in fairy tales and folk tales, like "The Pied Piper of Hamelin," and plays a "starring" role in Mozart's opera, *The Magic Flute.*

A musician can also modulate the sound by changing his embouchure and the angle of the air blown across the blow hole, creating faster or slower vibrations, which translate into higher or lower notes.

Without the blowhole there would be no sound from the flute, but there's more to this instrument than that! It is designed in three parts: the head joint, the body and the foot joint. It is on the head joint that you'll find the lip plate, which provides a rest for the lower lip on the blowhole. The head joint is also used by the player to tune the flute slightly higher or lower. The body is the center part of the flute, and this is where most of the instrument's 13 keys are found. Each one covers a hole, and the flutist covers and uncovers them to play different notes. Finally, the foot joint is what we call the opposite end of the head joint.

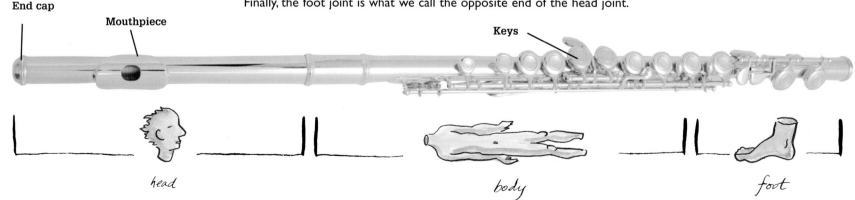

End cap

Mouthpiece

Keys

head

body

foot

PICCOLO

Piccolo means "little" in Italian.

The sound of the flute is made when the flautist blows air across the blowhole. Flautists "modulate" the sound (making it higher or lower) by pressing on the instrument's 13 keys, which shorten or lengthen the distance the vibrating air travels. These keys allow the player to play quick scales, making the flute a very versatile instrument.

The flautist plays his or her instrument by holding it up and to the side. When air is blown into the flute, the shape of the mouth, called the "embouchure" (pronounced ahm-boo-sure), is very important.

While the flute is one of the highest, the piccolo is the highest instrument in the orchestra. The piccolo is actually a short flute.

While it is only 1 foot long, this instrument makes a sound that is an entire octave higher than the standard flute and the sound rings out clearly above the rest of the orchestra. The flute is so similar to the piccolo that any flautist can play the piccolo.

If the flute is metal and it is being played in hot conditions, the pitch of the instrument rises as it becomes warmer. To fix this, the musician simply pulls the head joint out from the body a little to increase the length of the tube, and this lengthening causes the pitch of the instrument to rise.

The only other difference between the flute and piccolo besides the pitch and length is that the piccolo breaks down into two pieces rather than three for easier carrying when it is not being played.

Play Track 24 to hear the flute and its little cousin, the piccolo, play together in a piece of the third movement of Tchaikovsky's *Symphony No. 4*. At first, you'll hear the flute playing a simple theme for a while, then the piccolo—which sounds very much the same but much higher—happily chirping away.

Although there are bass and alto flutes that play lower tones, they rarely appear in orchestras, though they're often used in jazz bands.

The piccolo is half the length of the flute.

OBOE

QUACK!

The Instrument that the Orchestra Tunes By

The oboe was invented in the 17th century by Frenchmen Jean Hotteterre and Michel Danican Philidor. It is a wooden instrument whose sound is made by blowing through a double reed at the upper end of the instrument. An oboe's sound is quite strong, and once you know it, it is easy to pick out even when many of the orchestra's instruments are playing. It sounds a little like a long quack from a duck.

With its "reedy" sound, the oboe has a rather heartbroken, sad quality. Despite this, it is occasionally given the opportunity to be very playful, and, with its slightly nasal sound, even spiteful. Because the musician must force air at very high pressure into the tiny slice in the reed, the oboe is very difficult to play. The high pressure of the air as it is sent through the reed helps to create the oboe's unique, focused tone. Oboists create different pitches with the air being forced through the double reed by pressing the keys that cover holes in the body of the oboe.

Keys operated by the little fingers are very important on woodwind instruments. Pressing down on any of the little finger keys will open or close a hole farther down the instrument that the hands can't reach.

Double reed

The upper octave key controls the highest of the oboe's high notes. It is operated by the side of the left index finger.

The complex metal keywork makes the instrument surprisingly heavy!

The Cor Anglais

Just as the piccolo is similar to the flute, the cor anglais is very much like the oboe. Also known as the "English horn," the cor anglais is another double-reed instrument that can be played by oboists. Some people find the cor anglais very confusing, since it is neither English nor a horn.

The cor anglais is larger than the oboe, and plays a little lower than its cousin. The player often supports this rather heavy instrument on a sling around his neck. The cor anglais sounds wonderful in slow, thoughtful solos, and is often used to imitate a shepherd's pipe.

Because of this strength it is also the instrument that plays the tuning note to which all the members of the orchestra tune their instruments— usually an A—at the beginning of orchestra rehearsals and concerts.

Reed Making: An Oboe Player's Good Vibrations. Oboe players spend hours making their own reeds so that they can be sure that they match their playing style. Here's how it is done: The double reed is a narrow strip of cane that is scraped very thin, folded over double, and tied to a fine metal tube called a "staple." The fold is then cut through, leaving the two pieces of reed fixed closely together. When the player blows on the reed, the two pieces vibrate against each other. In this way they start the air in the tube vibrating, which creates sound.

Bell

Legend has it that years of playing the oboe can make you crazy because the vibrations from the high pressure of the air necessary to play the instrument are concentrated right in the middle of your forehead.

Play Track 25
on the CD to hear Tomaso Giovanni Albinoni's (say that three times fast!) *Sinfonia in G Major for Two Oboes.* At the beginning, you hear just the strings and the harpsichord (which sounds sort of like a cross between a piano and a harp), then one oboe comes in, then another. The second oboe dances along playfully with the first oboe, then the strings come back in. Listen through this piece as the oboes take turns with each other and the rest of the orchestra.

CLARINET

The Warm Tones of the Orchestra

The ligature holds reed in place.

Clarinets are played not only in orchestras, but also in marching and jazz bands. Made of wood or molded plastic, clarinets can be found in different sizes, each playing a different range of notes. The standard "B-flat" clarinet is a little more than 2 feet long. An orchestra also often includes an "E-flat" clarinet, which is smaller and plays a higher range of notes, and a bass clarinet, which plays an octave lower.

Like the oboist, the clarinetist blows into a reed that is clipped to the mouthpiece at the upper end of the instrument. The reed is made out of cane, like the oboes and cor anglais's, but it is a single reed, rather than a double reed. Also, like with the other woodwinds, the clarinetist plays different pitches by pressing on the clarinet's many keys. The bottom of the clarinet flares out into a bell shape, also like the oboe.

The sound that comes out of the bell-shaped end of the standard clarinet is a smooth, mellow tone. Clarinets have a large range of four octaves, from warm, low notes to a pure, clear upper register. Since the bass clarinet is so much larger, it is no surprise that it has a much lower sound, which gives it a mysterious quality.

The thumb rest is a small metal plate that helps the clarinetist support the weight of the instrument with the right thumb. (It's on the other side of the clarinet.)

The bass clarinet has a different shape from a standard clarinet. It is so much longer that it would be too awkward to play if its tube were straight, so the neck is bent, and the bell (the sound hole at the instrument's end) is curved around so that it faces up. Despite the size differences, it is still played the same way as the other members of its family.

The smooth warm tones of the clarinet come from its straight tubing.

Play Track 26
to hear the third movement of Mozart's *Concerto for Clarinet and Orchestra*. The clarinet was a relatively new instrument in the 1780s and Mozart seems to have fallen in love with it. In this, the last movement of his clarinet concerto (one of the last works he composed before his sad, early death at age 35), we can hear how he appreciated both the mellow and virtuoso aspects of the instrument, as he writes a sweet, yet fancy melody for it, and gets it to play at both ends of its considerable range.

SAXOPHONE

The Jazziest of the Orchestra Instruments

Patented in 1846 by Adolphe Sax, the saxophone is a hybrid of the clarinet and the oboe. The saxophone's single reed and mouthpiece is much like a clarinet, but its brass body and flared bell are unique in the woodwind section.

The bell of the saxophone flares out. The bells of alto, tenor and baritone saxophones are turned upward and lean slightly forward to help project the sound. Soprano saxophones have a bell that faces straight down, like a clarinet.

The ligature secures the reed in position.

The saxophone has a clarinet-like mouthpiece that fits onto the top of the instrument.

The saxophone has keys that extend over much of its length. Each key covers a tone hole.

There are four major types of saxophones, each playing a different range of notes. From highest to lowest, they are soprano, alto, tenor, and baritone. The sound these instruments make is both sweet and mellow, like the clarinet's, but it is strong, too, like the oboe's.

Soprano   Alto   Tenor   Baritone

THE SAXOPHONE FAMILY

The saxophone is supported using a combination of a thumb rest and a neck strap.

Although it was originally used in military marching bands, it was soon adopted into orchestras, and today the saxophone is most often associated with jazz.

Play Track 27
to hear a part of Maurice Ravel's *Bolero*. For the entire 16 minutes of the piece, different instruments play the main theme while snare drums maintain a steady rhythm. The part you are hearing now, where the saxophone takes its turn, comes not quite halfway through. Listen for the smooth, velvety sound of the alto sax, especially when it plays way down low. Then listen as a soprano sax, which is higher than the alto sax, plays the theme again, scooping and sliding around in the high notes.

BASSOON & CONTRA-BASSOON

The Wacky Woodwinds

The bassoon is another double-reed instrument, but this one is made of almost 8 feet of wood tubing, bent into a narrow U-shape, producing a weird and a little awkward shape.

Judging from the bassoon's size, it is not surprising to learn that playing the bottom notes of woodwind chords is one of the most important jobs of these instruments. They have a deep, dark, rich tone that inspired one poet to compare it to the sound of a sea god speaking.

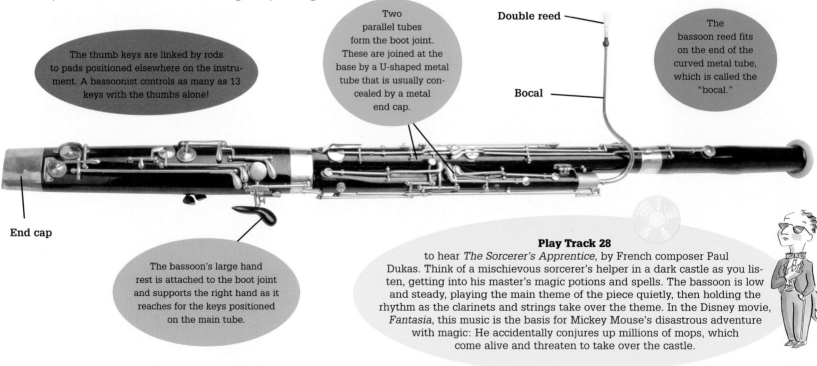

Two parallel tubes form the boot joint. These are joined at the base by a U-shaped metal tube that is usually concealed by a metal end cap.

The thumb keys are linked by rods to pads positioned elsewhere on the instrument. A bassoonist controls as many as 13 keys with the thumbs alone!

Double reed

Bocal

The bassoon reed fits on the end of the curved metal tube, which is called the "bocal."

End cap

The bassoon's large hand rest is attached to the boot joint and supports the right hand as it reaches for the keys positioned on the main tube.

Play Track 28
to hear *The Sorcerer's Apprentice*, by French composer Paul Dukas. Think of a mischievous sorcerer's helper in a dark castle as you listen, getting into his master's magic potions and spells. The bassoon is low and steady, playing the main theme of the piece quietly, then holding the rhythm as the clarinets and strings take over the theme. In the Disney movie, *Fantasia*, this music is the basis for Mickey Mouse's disastrous adventure with magic: He accidentally conjures up millions of mops, which come alive and threaten to take over the castle.

Because of the bassoon's low pitch, it rarely plays solos, but when it does, it can be quite fun to hear. While these passages are often short and choppy, bassoons can also play smooth, long melodies that are very expressive. To create this sound, the bassoon's tubular body is divided into four sections, which doubles back on itself to make it easier to play.

Since it is such a large instrument, the bassoonist holds the instrument to one side, next to his knee. He blows the reed in the same way an oboist player does. The bassoon's weight is usually supported by a seat strap, which the player hooks on to the lower end of the bassoon and then sits on. As you can guess, a bassoonist never stands up during a solo!

The pitch of a contrabassoon is so low that it seems to buzz.

The bell of the contrabassoon is made of metal.

It's just not fair...

You'd have to be 7 feet tall to play the bassoon if it weren't folded in half, and twice as tall to play the contrabassoon! Still, since they're so big and heavy, these instruments require a lot of work from the musician.

Thats huge!

#1 BIGGEST

As large as the bassoon is, it is not the largest instrument in the woodwind section: That would be the contrabassoon, which has 16 feet of wooden tubing and a metal bell. If it were straight, it would almost be as tall as a two-story house.

The spike that sticks out of its lower bend supports the con-trabassoon.

Play Track 29
to hear Maurice Ravel's interpreta-tion of a conversation between Beauty and the Beast. This piece, which is part of his *Mother Goose Suite*, features the contrabas-soon; listen for its deep, deep sound, answering after the first, lighter section. *The Mother Goose Suite* includes the tale of Sleeping Beauty, Hop-o'my-thumb and a Fairy Garden, especially for young audiences.

BRASS SECTION

As you might guess, the instruments in the brass section are usually made of metal, often brass. They are played with the air from the player and so they, too, are wind instruments and somewhat similar to the woodwinds. The difference between the two sections is that the musician who plays brass must use his or her lips, instead of the reed, to make the vibrations that make the sound.

Tensing his or her lips against the mouthpiece (which varies in design, depending on the instrument) and blowing through them, the musician makes his or her lips vibrate just like the double reed in an oboe does. This makes the air in the brass instrument vibrate and the tone differs depending upon how tense the player's lips are: Loose lips vibrate slowly and create low notes; tight lips vibrate quickly and produce high notes.

Brass instruments are really just long metal tubes that flare at one end. They are actually quite long, so the tubes are bent and folded into more compact shapes that are easier to hold. This portability, combined with their loudness and the fact that their tone carries a long way, is the reason why brass instruments are often used in marching bands.

Members of the brass family that play in the orchestra are the trumpet, the horn, the trombone and the tuba. Because of the strong sound this section creates it is in the back of the orchestra. Usually, an orchestra has one or two of each of these instruments, sometimes more.

A register is the range of an instrument or voice; in other words, how high and low the instrument can play.

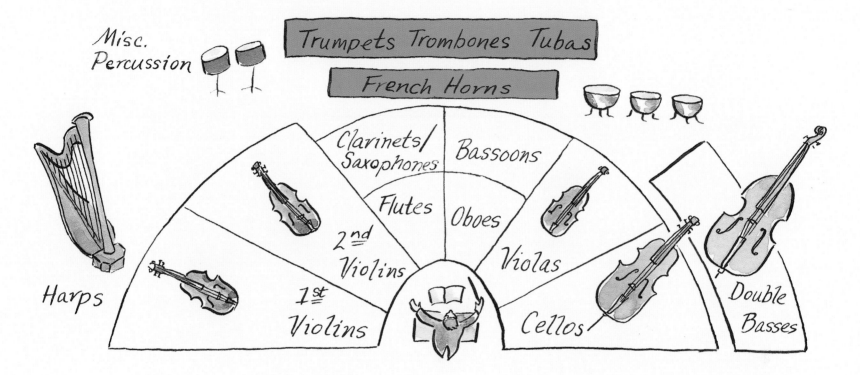

Misc. Percussion

Trumpets Trombones Tubas

French Horns

Clarinets/ Saxophones

Bassoons

Flutes

Oboes

2nd Violins

1st Violins

Violas

Harps

Cellos

Double Basses

The vibration of the lips used to play brass instruments is like a controlled "raspberry"—also known as a "Bronx cheer" when you are making fun of somebody.

Because playing lots of high notes in the upper limit of a brass instrument's register can be extremely exhausting to the musician's lips, there is usually an extra player—called a "bumper"—in the brass section to play when the other brass players are tired.

TRUMPET

The Bold, Loud Mouth of the Brass Section

If you have ever seen a movie in which a king is in his great hall, you have probably seen a trumpet—it's the instrument that those guys in the balcony are playing whenever something important happens or royalty enters. Trumpets are at least 3,500 years old—early versions were found in King Tut's tomb! The loud, clear sound of the trumpet has been used to send signals, frighten enemies in battle, and begin ceremonies with blazing fanfares. The trumpet is very popular with jazz musicians as well as orchestras.

Although they come in different sizes and lengths, the standard trumpet is the one that appears most often in the orchestra. The largest trumpet is the bass trumpet, and it's so big that occasionally trombone players play it instead of trumpeters. As it is, standard trumpets are 18 inches long, but if the tube were unwound, it would be 4 1/2 feet long, three times the length of the instrument!

The trumpet's mouthpiece is vital to producing its sound. It has a small, shallow, cup-shaped opening, against which the players must adjust the air pressure and shape of their lips to change the pitch of a note. To alter the overall pitch of the instrument, the player adjusts the tuning slide, which changes the length of the trumpet tube. When pressed in different combinations, the trumpet's three valves allow the trumpeter to play every note in the instrument's range.

"God tells me how the music should sound, but you stand in the way."
—Arturo Toscanini to a trumpet player in his orchestra

After playing for a while, the trumpet's sound can become "gurgly." This sounds gross, but it happens because the player's breath condenses inside the trumpet, forming drops of water. To fix this, the trumpeter presses the water key, which opens a hole in the tube allowing the water to drip out.

The bell of the trumpet sends the sound forward, helping to produce the full tone we expect from the trumpet. To change this sound a mute can be inserted into the bell.

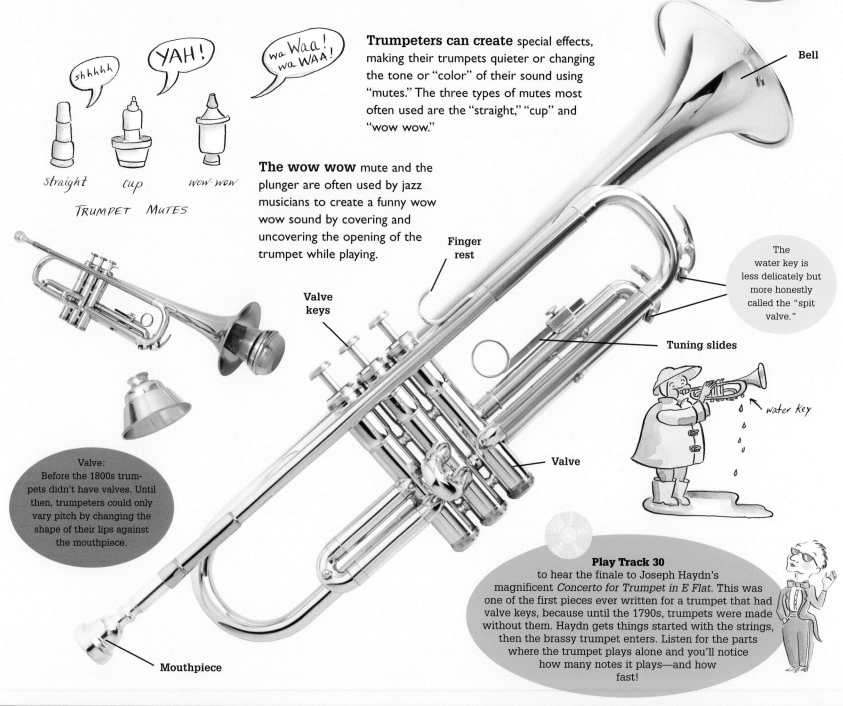

shhhhh

YAH!

wa Waa! wa WAA!

straight   cup   wow-wow

TRUMPET MUTES

Trumpeters can create special effects, making their trumpets quieter or changing the tone or "color" of their sound using "mutes." The three types of mutes most often used are the "straight," "cup" and "wow wow."

The wow wow mute and the plunger are often used by jazz musicians to create a funny wow wow sound by covering and uncovering the opening of the trumpet while playing.

When played full blast, the sound that comes out of this bell is a bold, bright, exciting one that can be heard over the whole orchestra.

Bell

Finger rest

Valve keys

The water key is less delicately but more honestly called the "spit valve."

Tuning slides

water key

Valve

Valve:
Before the 1800s trumpets didn't have valves. Until then, trumpeters could only vary pitch by changing the shape of their lips against the mouthpiece.

Mouthpiece

Play Track 30
to hear the finale to Joseph Haydn's magnificent *Concerto for Trumpet in E Flat*. This was one of the first pieces ever written for a trumpet that had valve keys, because until the 1790s, trumpets were made without them. Haydn gets things started with the strings, then the brassy trumpet enters. Listen for the parts where the trumpet plays alone and you'll notice how many notes it plays—and how fast!

FRENCH HORN

One of the Hardest Instruments to Master

A ncient French horns did not have valves. It would not be until the 1800s that the instrument took the shape it bears today. Before this, horns were simply one long piece of metal tubing coiled around into a circle that were used to remind listeners of hunting, so their role in the orchestra was limited. Once the valves were added, however, the instrument's versatility was discovered, and it has been in the orchestra ever since.

The French horn's velvety, mellow quality enables it to blend well with the orchestra. Its sound bridges the gap between the brass and the woodwind family.

The French horn is often used to blend the sounds of the woodwinds with the sounds of the brass section. It does this so well that it can be difficult to tell the difference between the horn and the bassoon. Most importantly, this sound crosses over, rather than overpowers, other instruments in the orchestra.

That is not to say that the horn does not have quite a scope of sound. Its tone can range from bold and brassy to soft and round. The horn has this range because of the conical tubing used in its construction— the tube becomes gradually wider as it approaches the bell. Knowing that the French horn has this great range makes it easy to understand why the instrument has been part of the orchestra for nearly 200 years.

Players are able to balance the instrument on their leg, while holding the instrument between both hands. A player's left hand works the valves that help change the horn's pitch, and his or her right hand is held inside the bell, allowing the volume, pitch and tone of the instrument to be varied by the manner in which the hand is moved.

Since it is difficult to master both the extreme high and low notes of the French horn, musicians often specialize in one range or another.

Play Track 31
In olden days a version of the French horn was very similar to the horn that people used when hunting. In this selection from the finale of Mozart's *Horn Concerto No. 1* you can hear what a difficult instrument the French horn is to play and can practically see the men, horses and hunting dogs chasing a fox.

Horns are even more ancient than trumpets. The first horns were made from the horns of animals, which give them their name. Primitive hunters discovered that they could break off the tip of the horn and blow into the hole to sound a note. Hunters used these to send signals to one another during their hunts.

The French horn is a surprisingly complicated instrument to play. While supporting the hefty instrument and adjusting the tone with the right hand, the player's left hand is also busy. The left thumb works a valve that allows two sets of tubing to be used. One of the sets is shorter and used for playing high notes, and the longer second set is used for low notes.

Fitting into the upper end of the tube, the size of the mouthpiece that players use depends upon whether they play high or low parts. If they play mostly lower parts, then they choose a wider and deeper mouthpiece. A narrower and shallower one is used if they play higher parts.

Bell

If the horn were not coiled, it would be 12 feet long, about as long as a car!

Mouthpiece

The horn bell has an extremely wide flare that is sometimes detachable. With their hand in the bell, players can vary the horn's sound and volume.

The thumb valve is used to cut a third of the tubing to raise the pitch of the horn.

Valve

The little finger of the left hand slips under the finger rest to help support the instrument, leaving the other fingers of the hand to operate the valves' levers.

When the three valve levers are pressed, they move rods that cause the valve to turn and allows air into an extra length of tubing and lowers the pitch of the note.

Valve leveler

The French horn is unique because the player actually puts his right hand in its bell, sometimes for support and sometimes for the following reason: Using a technique called "hand-stopping" the player can actually change how the instrument sounds. In the days before valves this made more notes available, but today, the dark metallic tone produced by these "stopped" notes is a device used by many composers for its own sound quality.

Most orchestras have four French horns working in two pairs—first and third taking the higher part, and second and fourth the lower part.

TROMBONE

The brassy sound of the trombone is helped by its widely flared bell.

The water key, also called the "Spit valve." Just like the trumpet, water can collect in the trombone giving it a bubbling sound when played. The spit valve allows players to blow in and dry out the instrument.

Water key

The slide is 2 feet long. By lengthening the slide the trombone player plays lower notes. Moving the slide back and shortening the instrument produces higher notes.

Slide-Action Trumpet But Lower

Trombones have been in orchestras for quite a while. They were invented in the 1400s (at the time they were called "sackbuts") as an improvement upon the trumpet. During this early period, before the invention of things like valves on brass instruments, sackbuts had slides that allowed the player to change the length of its tubing, and thus the pitch they were playing.

While it may not seem like much today, the invention of the slide was a vast improvement over other brass instruments in the 15th century. The modern trombone has come a long way since those early instruments (the tube is wider and the mouthpiece different), but players still push and pull a slide as they blow air into the mouthpiece to create sound. The vibrations of the player's lips—with varying degrees of tightness and air pressure—when pressed against the rim of the mouthpiece, combined with the manipulation of the slide, produce the trombone's rich, low voice.

Trombones form the middle harmony between the higher trumpets and lower tubas (see "Tuba," later). Trombones also play great solos and can produce an effect that no other instrument can imitate. This effect is called "glissando," and it is a change from one note to another quickly and smoothly, that is made possible by the player moving the slide while continuing to blow air through the mouthpiece. The effect can be comical—it can sound like a frown or a smile, depending on whether the player goes from high to low or vice-versa.

If the total length of the trombone were unwound, it would be 9 feet long and almost reach the ceiling in your house.

The term "sackbut," the name of the early trombone, comes from French *saquebute*, a type of lance with a hook that was used to pull things—the hook of the curved slide of what we now call a trombone reminded people of this hooked lance.

Most orchestras have three trombones, two tenor and one bass.

Tubing

The mouthpiece of the trombone has a deep cup-shape.

Tuning slide

Play Track 32
to hear Mahler's *Symphony No. 3*. At an epic one hour and 40 minutes, it was so big that it even scared him. "It is terrible, the way it keeps growing and expanding," he said of the first movement. The melody starts with the brassy trumpets, then the trombones come in with their ominous fanfare. When the trombones perform their downward slide two or three times in a row, you know that there's really something very serious, deep and heavy going on!

TUBA

I may be big but I'm nimble!

The Biggest and Lowest Brass

First used in military marching bands in the 1820s, about the time the camera was invented, the tuba is the youngest member of the brass section. It is also the largest member of the family and produces the lowest notes. Like the double basses and bassoons, the tuba is important to the orchestra for its deep, resonant sound.

Looking at a tuba, you would not be surprised at the deep, heavy sound it makes. It consists of a huge conical brass tube that bends around, beginning at the mouthpiece and ending with a large flared bell.

Similar to the French horn, the conical tubing gives the tuba a beautiful, mellow tone when it plays high notes. It does not, however, often get an opportunity to do this, as given the low pitch of the instrument, it is often difficult to hear it separate from the rest of the orchestra. When a composer does give the tuba an opportunity to play a solo, it is surprising to hear how nimble it is.

If you don't think that the tuba is a big instrument, just try unbending it: If you did, the tuba would be 18 feet long! Now that's a lot of metal.

Tubas actually have a very wide range of notes that can be played quite quickly.

Sousaphone

In the orchestra, musicians rest the tuba in their lap and blow into the mouthpiece while pressing different notes on the valves. Like the other members of the brass family, the manner in which the player blows air into the mouthpiece also affects the sound the instrument makes. If used in a marching band, the tuba player rests this big instrument on his or her shoulder. There is also a variation on the tuba called the sousaphone, which was invented by John Philip Sousa, the American composer and marching band leader, especially for marching bands. The tubing of the sousaphone wraps itself around the player so that it is much easier to carry.

The wide bell enables the tuba to project its sound outward and is upright, pointing at the ceiling.

The mouthpiece of the tuba has a very deep cup-shape.

The most high-pitched tuba is the tenor euphonium. It looks like a standard tuba but is smaller and sometimes has four valves instead of three. *Euphonium* means "well sounding" in Greek.

Unsurprisingly, the tuba's mouthpiece is very big and deep. It takes a lot of breath to play the tuba, but unlike other brass instruments you don't have to keep your lips tight or force your breath. Simply cushioning your loose lips against the deep, cup-shaped mouthpiece is enough!

There is a specially designed version of the tuba called the "recording" tuba, whose bell faces forward instead of upwards, projecting the sound more effectively toward the microphones of a recording studio.

Valves

Tubas have three valves, which lengthen the distance the air has to travel, thereby lowering the pitch of the note played.

Play Track 33
to hear *Pictures at an Exhibition*. In this work (orchestrated by Maurice Ravel from sketches by the composer, Mussorgsky) we're presented with musical impressions of just what the title says: pictures at an exhibition. In this one you'll hear a "Bydlo," or heavy cart pulled by oxen. Note how the tuba, even played high, can sound lumbering and heavy, but persistent—and sort of clumsy, the way oxen are.

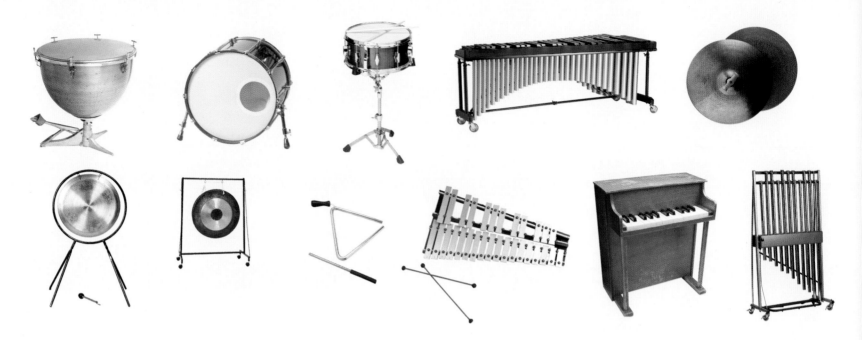

PERCUSSION SECTION

The section with the greatest variety of instruments in it is the percussion section. Included here are instruments that make a sound when banged, tapped or shaken. Although it might seem as if there would be a bunch of musicians here playing all of these different sorts of percussion instruments, there actually aren't. A percussionist may play many different instruments during a concert. In the percussion section, the triangle player usually doubles as tam-tam player and the bass drum player can play the snare drum, but the cymbalist only plays cymbals and the timpanist only plays timpani. Nowadays, there's occasionally someone called the "utility percussionist" who will play anything other than timpani. This works because the percussion instruments usually do not play at the same time.

Although the percussion section is found in the back of the orchestra, the rhythmic and colorful sounds it creates are able to carry out, over and through the sound made by the rest of the sections. Instruments found in the percussion section are really of two basic types. The simplest type, like the gong, is untuned and produces a note of indeterminate pitch. Tuned instruments, like the xylophone, are capable of playing melodies. Instruments found in these two groups of percussion instruments are the timpani, bass drums, snare drums, tubular bells, glockenspiels, gongs, triangles and xylophones.

Misc. Percussion

Trumpets Trombones Tubas

French Horns

Clarinets/Saxophones

Bassoons

Flutes

Oboes

2nd Violins

Violas

1st Violins

Cellos

Harps

Double Basses

Evelyn Glennie is the only full-time solo percussionist in the field of classical music, and she has won **44** awards, including a Grammy. This would be remarkable enough, but also she had been profoundly deaf since she was twelve years old! How does she do it? She distinguishes the pitch of notes by associating where on her body she feels the vibrations. She feels the low sounds mainly in her legs and feet and the high sounds might be particular places on her face, neck and chest. Amazing!!

Play Track 34
to hear almost every percussion instrument possible in Rodion Schedrin's *Carmen Suite*. This section is called "Changing of the Guard"—listen carefully, and you can picture soldiers, especially at the beginning. As the music continues, listen for different percussion sounds. You'll hear a snare drum, which sounds like a rattlesnake caught in a drum set, the sweet ringing of the triangle, the clanking cowbell, the tick-tock of the woodblock, the bell-like sound of the glockenspiel and the melodic beat of the xylophone. There are many, many percussion instruments in this piece, but Schedrin wrote it so that since there are only five people in the percussion section, each plays more than one instrument at different times.

Big Booming Copper Kettles

TIMPANI

Because they underline chords that the rest of the orchestra is playing, the most important percussion instrument in the orchestra is the timpani. You might say it is the pulse of the orchestra. Timpani are also called kettledrums because the bottom of the drums are large, deep bowls that are made from copper and are shaped like big copper kettles. Stretched across the top is a drumhead (also called the "head"), which is made from either calfskin or thin plastic.

When the skin is struck by a drumstick it can produce different notes because the head can be tightened or slackened by a mechanism operated by a foot pedal.

There are usually three or four timpani in a modern orchestra, each drum of a different size, and each one tuned to a different note.

When playing the timpani, the player strikes the drumhead with sticks called "beaters." There are actually several different types of beaters used, and each kind produces a different tone quality.

Egg beater   Self beater   Brow beater   Timpani beater

The timpani came from military marching bands of the 17th century. Originally smaller than they are today but still too large to be carried, they were slung on either side of a horse and played by a mounted bandsman.

Play Track 35
to hear the timpani bellow out the opening to the final movement of Gustav Mahler's *Symphony No. 7*. After the rest of the orchestra comes in, playing their joyous marching finale, you can still hear the timpani thundering away, with the cymbals as an exclamation point. On the score, Mahler instructed the timpanists to play *mit bravour*, which means "with bravery."

When the tension screws around the side of the drumhead are tightened, the head is stretched and the drum's pitch rises. When they are loosened, the pitch gets lower.

Stretched over the resonator is the drumhead, made of flexible calfskin or thin plastic.

On early versions of the timpani, the pitch could be changed by altering the tension of the head by a series of hand screws positioned around the circumference of the drum.

Timpanists do not hit the center of the head but rather 3 inches from the rim of the drum.

The kettle-shaped main chamber is called the "resonator." You could make a pretty big soup in there!

The timpanist uses a tuning gauge to set the pitch. Timpani that have these mechanisms are called "machine drums."

The player can change the pitch of a drum at will. He is often asked to change the pitch of a drum during the music to blend with the rest of the orchestra. Thus the player is often seen operating the pedal and putting his ear close to the drumhead as he tests the pitch by flicking it with his finger or striking it gently with a drumstick.

The pedal at the foot of the resonator is used to adjust the tension screws, which tightens or loosens the drumhead.

BASS & SNARE DRUMS

The bass and snare drums are the stalwarts of the percussion section. The bass drum is the largest of the drums and the snare is the smallest. They came to the orchestra from military marching bands.

Being the largest drum in the orchestra, the bass drum's tone is very low and deep, which should come as no surprise. This big, round cylinder has drumheads on both sides, and it is played upright. In the orchestra the bass drum sits on a stand, but in a marching band it is carried by the drummer on a harness.

Hole to let the sound out

While the sound this drum makes can be booming—a soft drumroll can sound like distant thunder—it can also be played quite quietly.

Drum stick

The snares are at the bottom of the drum.

The tension screws around the rim keep the head tight.

The snare switch enables the drummer to turn off the snares.

The stand holds the snare drum in place.

Also shaped like a cylinder, the snare drum is small enough that in a marching band the drummer can carry it on his or her waist and play it off to the side, which is why it is also known as the "side drum." The snare drum's drumhead is stretched across the top of the cylinder, and it has a set of wires strung across the bottom of the instrument that produces the rattling sound. These wires are the "snare."

Drummers use different types of drumsticks, or beaters: Timpani sticks, soft-headed bass drumsticks, snare drumsticks or wire brushes.

Snare drummers can also turn off the snare to make a dull thud sound when they strike their drumhead.

When a bass drum has only one head, it is called a "gong drum." The gong drum looks like a huge tambourine without the metal jingles.

The drumroll that the snare drum makes is quite distinctive. It is produced when the player strikes the drum very rapidly bouncing both sticks one after the other. Besides this, the snare drum is capable of playing all sorts of other cool rhythms.

The Piano of the Percussion Section

Nobody is sure where the xylophone originated, but the earliest written reference to it comes from Mali in West Africa in the 14th century. Since that time it has become the most important tuned instrument in the percussion section. Its bright, dry and hard sound rings out across the orchestra.

The modern version of the instrument is based on the one used by 19th-century, traveling xylophone players who wandered Europe. Xylophones consist of a set of wooden bars, mounted on a frame, each tuned to a different pitch. They are arranged like a piano keyboard. The keys that would be white on a piano are on the front of the xylophone and those that would be the black ones are behind them in the frame.

Xylophone comes from the Greek, *xylo* meaning "wood" and *phone* meaning "sound."

The player strikes the bars with beaters to create its sound, and with the various keys, he or she is able to produce a great range of pitches. To really create the range of sound the xylophone is able to make, players use a wide array of beaters. For example, when struck with a hard beater, the xylophone creates a bright and sharp sound, while soft beaters make a gentler sound.

XYLOPHONE

Whether the xylophone comes from Africa or Asia is uncertain, but in Java and Bali a form of xylophone with keys resting on cloth and placed over a wooden trough is commonly associated with the gamelan ensemble, an Indonesian-style orchestra.

Made from rosewood, the bars of the xylophone are different sizes: Shorter bars play the higher notes; longer ones play lower notes.

On the largest xylophones there are as many as 50 wooden bars.

The wooden keys and resonators are held within the wheeled frame.

There is a metal tube, called the resonator, beneath each bar. Tuned to the same pitch as the bar above it, the air inside the bar vibrates when the bar is struck, which helps to project and sustain its sound.

The keys are connected to the frame by cords that pass through each one of them, holding them off the frame and permitting them to vibrate freely.

CYMBALS, GONGS &

Cymbals

Cymbals are brass discs, which curve inward.

The player holds each cymbal through a strap attached to the center of the outside part of the disc.

Cymbals, gongs and tam-tams are all percussion instruments that are similar to one another: They are each metal discs of various sizes. Despite looking alike, they have sounds that are very special to each of them.

Cymbals are two thin brass plates that the player clashes together to create a bright, sparkling crash often used in the finale of a big orchestral work to create excitement.

When the cymbals smash together, the edges of the plates (they are not flat but concave, so only the edges touch when brought together) vibrate creating a crashing sound.

SMASH! SMASH! I LOVE TO SMASH!

Smashing the cymbals together is not the only way to create sound, though. The musician can make them sweep past each other with a violent swish, or gently brush one with the other, making a more delicate sound. Sometimes the player will hold one cymbal and hit it with a soft stick; he or she can also mount one on a stand and play a roll with two sticks that creates a wonderful, delicate, shimmering sound.

Play Track 36
to hear the crashing cymbals in the finale to Pyotr Tchaikovsky's *Symphony No. 4.* Tchaikovsky uses the cymbals to mark the most energetic point in the music. Often, they are accompanied by the timpani and the string sections racing fast and furious up and down. As the music continues, the cymbals come in only at the loudest and most exciting parts, crashing in above the rest of the orchestra like a clap of golden, shimmering thunder.

Gong

The gong and tam-tam have come to the orchestra from the Far East. They are usually made of a copper-tin mixture. The gong (about 3 feet in diameter) is often smaller than the tam-tam (as large as 5 feet in diameter), but they are both larger than cymbals (about 1.5 feet in diameter). They are played with a heavy beater covered with felt or wool. The best way to tell them apart, however, is by their sounds: The gong makes a "bong" and the tam-tam a "crash."

Life is so different when you have pitch...

Bong, bong, bong...

CRASH!

Besides size, the main difference between the gong and tam-tam is that the edges of the gong are usually bent over, but the tam-tam's aren't.

The finale of a piece is the end or near the end of the musical work where all the melodies come to a dramatic and often uproarious climax. It comes from Italian and means the finish or end.

The gong uses a large beater to create its big bong.

The tam-tam hangs from the frame and is free to reverberate and crash.

TAM-TAMS

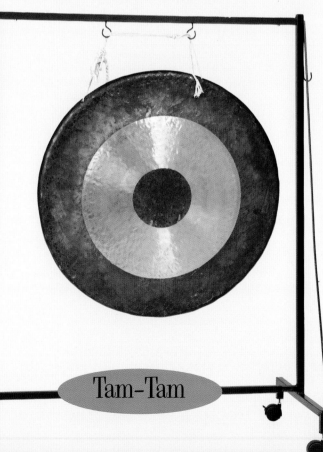

Tam-Tam

TRIANGLE

The Ding and Ping of the Orchestra

Triangles have been used since ancient times, and it was in the 18th century that it joined the orchestra. While it may be small, it is certainly an important member of the percussion section. This instrument is a simple steel rod bent into the form of a triangle, with one corner open.

The player creates sound by striking the triangle with a metal bar, called a beater. The triangle's pitch is not distinct and its tone varies depending on how hard it is struck, and the actual loudness of the instrument depends upon its size. Big triangles are louder than smaller ones, with the instrument ranging from 4 inches to 10 inches on each side.

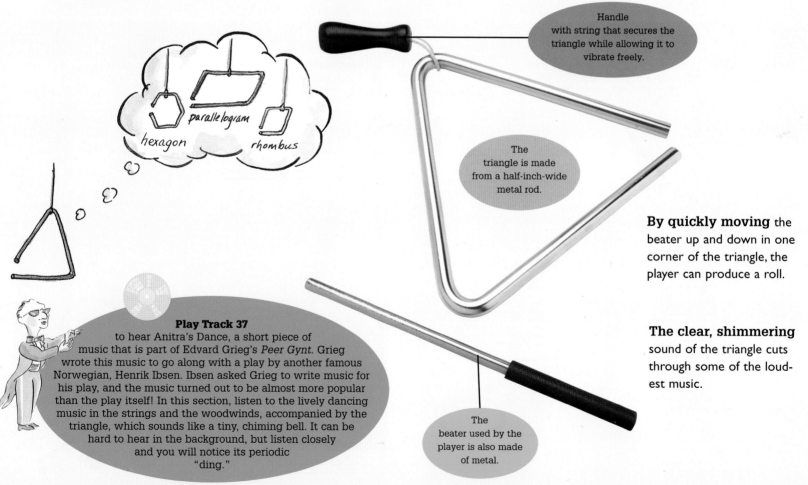

hexagon   parallelogram   rhombus

Handle with string that secures the triangle while allowing it to vibrate freely.

The triangle is made from a half-inch-wide metal rod.

By quickly moving the beater up and down in one corner of the triangle, the player can produce a roll.

The clear, shimmering sound of the triangle cuts through some of the loudest music.

Play Track 37 to hear Anitra's Dance, a short piece of music that is part of Edvard Grieg's *Peer Gynt*. Grieg wrote this music to go along with a play by another famous Norwegian, Henrik Ibsen. Ibsen asked Grieg to write music for his play, and the music turned out to be almost more popular than the play itself! In this section, listen to the lively dancing music in the strings and the woodwinds, accompanied by the triangle, which sounds like a tiny, chiming bell. It can be hard to hear in the background, but listen closely and you will notice its periodic "ding."

The beater used by the player is also made of metal.

The following three members of the percussion section produce sounds that are very much like bells. Despite the similarity of the sounds they make, each one is played quite differently from the others.

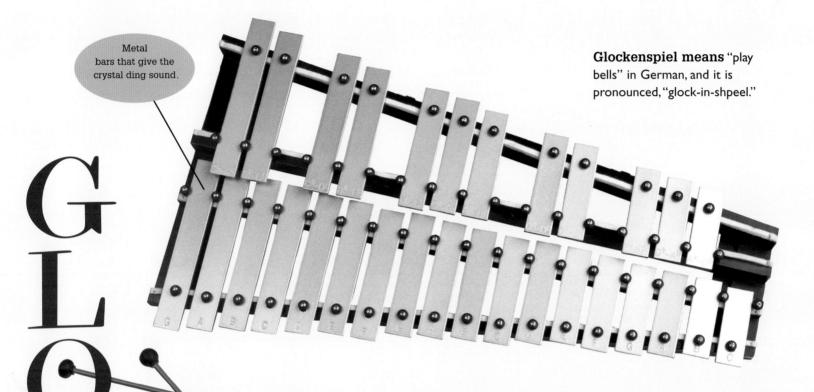

Metal bars that give the crystal ding sound.

Glockenspiel means "play bells" in German, and it is pronounced, "glock-in-shpeel."

Beater

GLOCKENSPIEL

The bell-like sound of the glockenspiel is made in the same way as the xylophone except its bars are made of metal and not wood. The modern instrument has a set of tuned steel bars arranged in two rows like the black-and-white notes of a piano keyboard. Glockenspiels are played with very hard beaters to produce a bell-like tone, and they may have a foot-operated damping mechanism or movable suspension to reduce resonance.

A Metal Xylophone

CELESTA

If the Glockenspiel and Piano Had a Child

In 1886 Auguste Mustel invented the celesta, or celeste, which is a keyboard glockenspiel. Similar to a piano, there are metal bars inside the celesta that are struck by felt-covered hammers from below when the black-and-white keys are pushed. Unlike the standard glockenspiel, each bar has its own box resonator that amplifies the tone of the instrument. Despite these resonators, the celesta's tone is not very strong so it is not a standard orchestral instrument. Nevertheless, the celesta's delicate, silvery sound is less hard than the glockenspiel's, and some composers prefer it.

CELESTA'S FAMILY TREE

GRANNY GLOCKENSPIEL · GRANDPOP PIANO

ME! (CELESTA)

Play Track 38
to hear the celesta playing the lovely "Dance of the Sugar Plum Fairy," from Tchaikovsky's *Nutcracker Suite*. The celesta is the sweet, bell-like sound that carries the melody. Although the celesta sounds like bells, it looks more like a piano.

TUBULAR BELLS

Elegant Church Bell Sounds

The player strikes the top of the tube to produce sound.

The tubular bells are tuned metal tubes of various lengths that are hung in a frame. The standard instrument has 18 tubes. These tubes produce a sound like church bells and are used whenever a score calls for this effect. This sound is produced when the player hits the tubes with a the beater.

Beater

The length of each tube affects the tone it produces.

A foot-operated damping mechanism can be used to stop the reverberations of the tubes and moderate the sound.

KEYBOARD INSTRUMENTS

Keyboard instruments such as the piano, harpsichord and organ, despite the fact that they do not have an "official" place, often appear in orchestras because of their importance to orchestral music. In music of the 16th and 17th centuries a harpsichord, small organ or pianoforte (the forefather of the piano as we know it) were used to underline the music harmonically and rhythmically, and often the orchestra would be led from the keyboard. They later became the favorite solo instruments of composers and performers alike, and hundreds of concertos and chamber pieces were composed for them.

There is no "keyboard" section in the orchestra.

ORGAN

The King of Instruments

The organ is an air-driven instrument consisting of one or more rows of individual pipes.

When the player presses the keys on the keyboard, valves inside the instrument release pressurized air into the pipes, which then emit a sound based upon the pipe's width and length. This is called "scaling." For example, a narrow pipe produces a sound more focused and more penetrating than wide-scaled ones. On a large organ, the sounds emitted are almost as varied as those of a modern-day synthesizer: Some of the pipes can sound like flutes, some like trumpets, and so on. Perhaps this is why the organ is known as "The King of Instruments."

As complicated and high-tech as it sounds, the organ was actually the first keyboard instrument. The invention of the pipe organ is credited to Ctesibius, an engineer who lived in Alexandria, Egypt, in the third century B.C.

Many organs are huge, taking up an entire wall of a church or symphony hall.

May I play, too?

Play Track 39
to hear Bach's *Toccata and Fugue in D Minor*. A toccata is a free-style, big composition for organ or harpsichord, and here, in this very famous one, the organ sounds as if it is announcing the entrance of a vampire, a haunted castle, or some other scary thing—in fact, it's been used in plenty of horror movies just to let the viewers know they're in for some kind of trouble.

After the third century, organs disappeared from western Europe, but in the ninth century they were reintroduced from Byzantium. When the organ was produced in Byzantium, air bellows replaced the water pumps. The air was pumped into the organ by a couple of kids who were hired to jump up and down on the bellows. When they got tired, the organist either had to stop playing or adjust his playing for the change in volume or pitch that the reduced airflow caused. These impressive instruments—they were considered cutting-edge technology, after all—were given as gifts to kings by the Byzantine emperors, and by the tenth century, they began to appear in churches.

In the last 1000 years, organs have continued to be considered important as both solo and orchestral instruments, but with the invention of the harpsichord they lost some of their importance within the orchestra.

This early instrument was activated by water rather than by air.

By the second century A.D. the Romans were using organs in theaters and in the Coliseum just as we hear organs at baseball games today.

J. S. Bach was more famous during his lifetime as an organist than he was as a composer, and some of his most important works were written for the organ.

PIANO

The Tool of the Composer

The first pianos were made by Bartolomeo Cristofori, who began work on them in 1698. He called his invention the "harpsichord with loud and soft." From this very long name, the piano became known as the "pianoforte" because, unlike the harpsichord, the player could control its softness (*piano* in Italian) and loudness (*forte* in Italian) with the amount of pressure applied to the keys.

People eventually shortened the name even more and today we know this instrument simply as the piano. The first pianos were built as early as the 1720s, and Bach is known to have tried playing one.

When the pianist, who sits on a stool in front of the keyboard, hits a key, hammers inside of the frame strike the strings, creating its wide range of soft and loud notes. Its strings are encased in a wooden frame with a keyboard attached.

Another thing that differentiates pianos from earlier keyboard instruments is the presence of pedals. The modern concert piano has two or three pedals. The one on the right (the sustaining pedal) removes the dampers from the strings, giving added duration and resonance to the sound, even though the hands have been removed from the keys. The one on the left (the soft pedal) reduces the volume by shifting all the hammers sideways so that they strike the strings from a closer position—this diminishes their impact. There is a middle pedal, which is not on all pianos. It is called the "sostenuto" pedal and allows the player to sustain a selected group of notes while still dampening the remaining strings. More rarely, the third pedal is a muffling device used when the player is practicing.

Play Track 40
In this movement from Beethoven's "Moonlight" Sonata, it is easy to hear how the sonata got its nickname. The arpeggios (an arpeggio is a chord, played note by note, rather than together) the pianist plays are as placid and still as the reflection of moonlight on a still lake. Later in the sonata, the mood changes drastically, but here, at the start, it's all beautiful peace.

The piano has strings just like the harpsichord, but these are struck by rebounding hammers rather than plucked as they are in that older keyboard instrument.

Composers use the piano to write their music because they can play several notes at once and hear how the music written for different instruments will sound together.

The piano took the harpsichord's place as the dominant keyboard instrument during the Romantic era.

Strings that make the sound.

The bridge holds the strings.

Black keys play the sharp and flat notes of the scale. The white keys play all the other notes.

Keys, usually made of ivory or plastic.

Which pedal!?

soft pedal

"sostenuto" pedal

sustaining pedal

Pianoforte means soft/loud, which was the original name for the piano because it could play quietly and with great volume.

HARPSICHORD

Although it, too, is operated by a keyboard, the harpsichord is quite different from the pipe organ. The harpsichord is a stringed keyboard instrument whose strings are, like a harp, plucked rather than struck, as they are inside a piano. Although not as old as the organ, there are references to harpsichords in art and writing from 600 years ago.

Because they did not need all those pipes and air and space like an organ, harpsichords became very popular.

**Looks Like a Piano
But Plays Like a Harp**

In the olden days, one had to be a king or a churchman to afford an organ. Harpsichords, however, were far less expensive and could fit easily into the home.

Play Track 41
Normally, when we think of the harpsichord, we think of very proper men and women in powdered wigs in an 18th-century room with candles, etc. Well, listen to a bit of the 3rd movement of Francis Poulenc's (1899-1963) *Concerto Champêtre* (which means "country-side") for a somewhat different approach. It begins with a solo for the harpsichord imitating a Baroque type of dance but soon, Poulenc's love for percussion, odd rhythms and just sheer playfulness take over. It's jumpy and nervous—and fun!

The harpsichord remained in use up to the late 18th century as a solo instrument and in orchestras, but after 1810 it fell out of use; the introduction of the piano, whose stronger sound is better able to keep up with larger, contemporary orchestras, caused the harpsichord to become outmoded. Since the 1880s the harpsichord has begun to reappear in contemporary orchestras, as modern versions of the instrument incorporate an iron frame holding thick strings at high tension, which enable them to better hold their own in the orchestra.

The harpsichord can only play at one volume level.

THE
Follow the Leader
CONDUCTOR

The person who leads the orchestra, standing between the musicians and the audience, is the conductor. In the modern orchestra, the conductor not only keeps time and makes sure that each section sounds as it should when performing a piece of music, but it is also his or her job to make sure the music comes across to the audience as the composer originally intended it. This is much harder than it sounds. Much of the music played by orchestras is by composers who are no longer around to make their intentions clear, and what is written—for example, time markings, length of notes, softness and loudness, the emphasis to be given to individual instruments when all are playing at once—is not as precise as it should be and is open to variations and interpretations.

Carl Maria von Weber was the composer/conductor who invented many of the things we take for granted in the orchestra today. Amongst them is his manner of standing in front of the orchestra at a podium (instead of off to the side or from the piano) and using the light white baton that we still see today. The lightness of the modern baton is important because it allows conductors to use subtle and graceful gestures when they are leading subtle and graceful music.

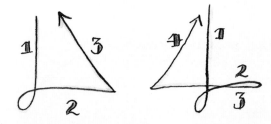

The conductor uses different patterns to mark the beat. When the music requires three beats per measure, the conductor waves the tip of the baton in the pattern to the far left, if it's four beats per measure he or she uses the pattern to the near left.

The score is the music the conductor reads off and it has all the parts for all the instruments listed on it.

Given that there is often such a great period of time between the creation of a composition and its performance, the conductor may change the way the music is played for a modern audience or because he simply thinks it sounds better his way. Also, music composed for a hall that seated 200 people and used very few instruments may have to be filled out to be appreciated (or just heard!) in the much larger halls that have been built since.

Back in the Baroque and Classical eras, conductors were simply musical servants in the court of a wealthy and powerful aristocrat or churchman. Their jobs ranged from writing music for special events to leading the court's orchestra (usually not more than 24 players) when it played music during their boss's dinner parties or for after-dinner entertainment. It was really in the Romantic Era that composers began to be stars in their own right, and with the rise of orchestras that were not dependent upon a king or bishop, the role of the conductor also began to look similar to what it is today.

In order to become a conductor, one does not have to know how to play every instrument, but how to read the music for each, i.e: what each instrument is capable of and how it translates from the written note to sound. Most conductors are trained pianists first (or trained in some instrument) and then decide to specialize in conducting. He or she must know what all of the composers' intentions were, how to read the markings on the score (soft, loud, with a bow, plucked, different speeds) and must learn how to "cue" the individual sections of the orchestra while also keeping in mind the "architecture" of the whole piece and how it all sounds when ALL the instruments are playing at the same time. Only years of experience can make a truly great conductor.

Chamber music of the Baroque Era did not have a formal conductor, the job of leading the orchestral ensemble was given to the first violinist or the harpsichord player. Sometimes there would be a conductor who would stand off to the side of the orchestra and use a rod or even pound the ground with a staff. Believe it or not, this last method could be dangerous—Jean Baptiste Lully, the favorite composer/conductor of King Louis XIV of France—liked to beat time with a big, heavy staff, and he accidentally pounded the staff on his foot instead of on the ground. The wound became infected with gangrene and the infection eventually killed him!

Unsurprisingly, most composers were also conductors. After all, who is better at making sure that the music sounds as it should than the person who wrote it?

I really like being in the center!

INDEX

LIST OF MUSICAL SELECTIONS

Photo Credits
All photographs licensed from Photodisk except for the cymbals, p70 and p78, celesta, p70 and p82, tubular bells, p70 and p83, and organ, p85 and p87 that are from Conrad & Company, Seattle WA and the contrabassoon, p59 provided by Fox Products Corporation.

Every effort has been made to clear the rights for all the musical selections and photographs.